Heck's
Pictorial Archive of
Military Science,
Geography and History

EDITED BY

J. G. HECK

DOVER PUBLICATIONS, INC.
NEW YORK

Bibliographical Note

This Dover edition, first published in 1994, contains the complete sections "Geography and Planography," "History," "Ethnology," "Military Sciences" and "Naval Sciences" (208 plates) and the accompanying descriptive contents of the plates from the *Iconographic Encyclopædia of Science, Literature, and Art. Systematically Arranged by J. G. Heck, Translated from the German, with Additions, and Edited by Spencer F. Baird, A.M., M.D., Professor of Natural Sciences in Dickinson College, Carlisle, PA. Illustrated by Five Hundred Steel Plates, Containing Upwards of Twelve Thousand Engravings*, originally published by Rudolph Garrigue, Publisher, New York, in 1851. The table of contents has been slightly rearranged for this edition.

DOVER *Pictorial Archive* SERIES

Library of Congress Cataloging-in-Publication Data

Heck, J. G. (Johann Georg), d. 1857.
   [Bilder Atlas zum Conversations Lexicon. English. Selections]
   Heck's pictorial archive of military science, geography, and history / edited by J. G. Heck.
      p.   cm. — (Dover pictorial archive series)
   A selection of engravings from the 1851 English ed., entitled Iconographic encyclopaedia of science, literature, and art, which was a translation of J. G. Heck's Bilder Atlas zum Conversations Lexicon.
   ISBN 0-486-28290-2
   1. World history—Pictorial works. 2. Military history—Pictorial works. 3. Engraving—19th century. I. Title. II. Title: Pictorial archive of military science, geography, and history. III. Series.
D21.1.H37213 1994
902'.2'2—dc20   94-25894
                                                                                 CIP

Manufactured in the United States of America
Dover Publications, Inc., 31 East 2nd Street, Mineola, N.Y. 11501

Contents

GEOGRAPHY AND PLANOGRAPHY

[Including a complete glossary of all those German geographical names and terms on the plates, which vary from the English, comprising also the *modern* names of *ancient* places, rivers, &c. The Longitude in the Maps is reckoned from the meridian of Ferro. To reduce it to the meridian of Greenwich add 18° 10' for W. long., and subtract the same for E. long.]

PLATE 1.
Physical map of Europe

PLATE 2, 3.
Mountain and river systems of Central Europe

PLATE 4.
Physical map of Asia

PLATE 5.
Physical map of Africa

PLATE 6.
Physical map of North America

PLATE 7.
Physical map of South America

PLATE 8.
I. Map of the world according to Herodotus
II. Map of the world according to Strabo,
III.   "   "   "   Ptolemy
IV. Map of the world known to the Ancients
V. Wind-chart of Aristotle
VI.   "   "   Vitruvius

PLATE 9.
The kingdom of Alexander the Great

PLATE 10.
Roman Empire under Constantine the Great,

PLATE 11.
Europe in the time of Charlemagne

PLATE 12.
Europe at the time of the Crusades

PLATE 13.
Europe before the French Revolution of 1789

PLATE 14, 15.
The railroads of Central Europe

PLATE 16.
Europe as it is at present

PLATE 17.
The Austrian Empire

PLATE 18.
Prussia

PLATE 19.
Denmark, Sweden, and Norway

PLATE 20.
Great Britain and Ireland

PLATE 21.
Spain and Portugal

PLATE 22.
France

PLATE 23.
Switzerland

PLATE 24.
Italy

PLATE 25.
Russia

PLATE 26.
The Turkish Empire

PLATE 27.
Greece

PLATE 28.
Asia

PLATE 29.
Africa

PLATE 30.
North America

PLATE 31.
South America

PLATE 32.
Australia

PLATE 33.
London

PLATE 34.
Paris and environs

PLATE 35.
Fortifications of Paris

PLATE 36.
Constantinople

PLATE 37.
St. Petersburg
Warsaw

PLATE 38.
Berlin

PLATE 39.
Vienna

PLATE 40.
Lisbon
Naples

PLATE 41.
Rome
Milan

PLATE 42.
Madrid
Saragossa
Barcelona

PLATE 43.
Copenhagen
Stockholm
Antwerp
Amsterdam

PLATE 44.
Leghorn
Florence
Ancona
Modena

GLOSSARY TO THE GEOGRAPHICAL MAPS.

Abasgia, Abkhas.
Abassien, Abassi (tribe in North Africa).
Abbitibes, Abbitibbe River.
Abdera, Adra.
Abrincate, Abrincafui.
Abyssinien, Abyssinia.
Acci, Guadix.
Achalziche, Akalzike.
Achen, Aix la Chapelle.
Acincum, Buda Pest.
Adagk, Island Adack.
Admiralitäts Is., Admiralty Islands.
Adrianopel, Adrianople.
Adriatisches Meer, Adriatic Sea.
Adulis, St. Gothard.
Ægadische In., the islands of Levanso, Favignana, and Maritimo (the ancient Ægades).
Ægäisches Meer, Archipelago.
Aegypten, Egypt.
Ægyptische Schöne wovon 18⁴⁄₅ *a. d. Gr.*, Egyptian miles 18⁴⁄₅ to a degree.
Ælana, Akaba.
Æmona, Laybach.
Æquat. d. ewigen Schnees, Equator of perpetual snow.

Æquatorgrenze d. Schneefalles, Equatorial boundary of snow.
Æquatorialgrenze d. europ. tropn. Getreides, Equatorial boundary of European tropical grain.
Æquatorialgr. des ewigen Schnees, Equatorial boundary of perpetual snow.
Æthiopien, Ethiopia.
Æthiopisches Meer, Ethiopian Sea.
Agrigentum, Girgenti.
Aguja Sp., Cape Aguya.
Akjerman, Akerman.
Alands In., Aland Islands.
Alanen, Alani.
Albanien, Albany.
Albaracin, Albarracin.
Albersche, Alberche River.
Albis, Elbe River.
Albufeira, Albufera.
Albufera See, Lake Albufera.
Alemannen, Alemanni.
Aleschki, Aleshki.
Aleuten Inseln, Aleutian Islands.
Alexandrien, Alexandria.
Algesiras, Al Gezira.
Algier, Algiers.
Alpen 1200 *t. mittlere Höhe*, Alps 1200 toises mean height.
Alpen Gebirge, the Alps.
Alpes Bastarnicæ, Lower Alps.
Alpes Rhætiæ, Rhætian Alps.
Alsen, Isle of Als.
Alt Californien, Upper California.
Alter Molo, Old pier.
Amassera, Amasserah.
Amboser Hochland, Ambose Highlands.
Amenis, Ameni Island.
Amiranten I., Amirante Islands.
Amisia, Ems River.
Ammonia, Hargiah.
Ancyra, Angora.
Andalusien, Andalusia.
Andamanen, Andaman Islands.
Andes von Peru, the Andes of Peru.
Andes von Quito, the Andes of Quito.
Andöe, Island of Andoen.
Andros mit Hafen, Andros with port.
Anemurium, Cape Anamour.
Angeln, Angli.
Anten, Antæ (Sarmatian tribe).
Antinoe, Enseneh.
Antwerpen, Antwerp.
Anurigrammum, Anurajapoera.
Aornus, Ohund.
Aosta Thal, Aosta Valley.
Apeliotes (Ost), Southeast trade-wind.
Apenninen Geb., the Apennines.
Apulien, Apulia.
Aquæ Sextiæ, Aix.
Aquitanien, Aquitania.
Arabien, Arabia.
Arabische Wüste, Arabian Desert.
Arab. Mb., Arabian Gulf.
Arabisches od. Persisches Meer, Arabian or Persian Sea.
Arachosia, S. E. Cabul.
Arachotus, Lora River.
Aral See, Aral Sea.
Aran, Karabagh.
Araxes, Aras River.
Arbela, Arbay.
Archangelsk, Archangel.
Archipel von Neu Britannia, Archipelago of New Britain.
Archipel der Niedrigen Inseln, Low Islands.
Archipelagus, Archipelago.
Ardennen, Ardennes.
Arelate, Arles.
Argolische In., Archipelago of Nauplia.
Argelis, Argellez.
Argentoratum, Strasbourg.
Argonnen Wald, the Argonne Forest.
Aria, Khorasan.

Aria See, Lake of Zarrah.
Ariaspæ, Ariaspes (inhabitants of Aria, in ancient Drangiana, in Persia.
Ariminum, Rimini.
Armenier, Armenians.
Armoricum, ancient Aquitania (S. W. France).
Arnheim, Arnhem.
Aroe, Patras.
Arsanus, Murad River.
Arsinoe, Suez.
Art. Magazin, Artillery Arsenal.
Aru In, Aroo Islands.
Arvernum, Auvergne.
Asiatisches Russland, Asiatic Russia.
Asiatisches Sarmatn., Asiatic Sarmatia.
Asow, Azov.
Asowsches Meer, Sea of Azov.
Assomtion, Asuncion.
Assyrn., Assyria.
Asta, Asti.
Asturica, Astorga.
Asturien, Asturias.
Athabasca S., Lake Athapescow.
Athen, Athens.
Athenæ, Athens.
Athribis, Tel Atrib.
Atlantischer Ocean, Atlantic Ocean.
Atschin, Acheen.
Attalia, Adalia.
Attici, Inhab. of Attica.
Augila, Augela.
Aug. Turinorum, Turin.
Aug. Vindelicorum, Augsburg.
Augustodunum, Autun.
Aulona, Valona.
Auster (Süd), South Wind.
Australien, Australia.
Austral. Busen, Gulf of Australia.
Austrasien, Empire of Chlodwig.
Avalites, Zeyla.
Avalitischer G., Bay of Zeyla.
Aventicum, Avenche.
Avernum, Lake Averno.
Azania, Ajan.
Azorische Inseln, Portugiesisch, the Azores, Portuguese.
Azowsches Meer, Sea of Azov.

B. von Athen od. v. Ægina, Bay of Athens or of Ægina.
B. von Nauplia od. v. Argos, Bay of Nauplia or of Argos.
Babadagh, Baba Dag.
Bagistanus, Beesitoon.
Bagous Geb., Bagous Mountains.
Bahama Inseln, Bahama Islands.
Bai u. Dorf Catalan, Bay and village of Catalan.
Baiern, Bavaria.
Baikal S. u. Geb., Baikal Lake and Mountains.
Baireuth, Bayreuth.
Bairischer Wd., Bavarian Forest.
Baktrien, Bactriana.
Balearen, Balearic Islands.
Baleares, Balearic Islands.
Balearischer Canal, Balearic Channel.
Balkan Geb., Balkan Mountains.
Balkasch S., Lake Balkash.
Baltica, Sweden.
Banasa, Mehedıma.
Banater Geb., Banat Mountains.
Banater Milit. Grenge, Military frontier of the Banat.
Banks Land, Banks' Island.
Barcelonnetti, Barceloneta.
Barcino, Barcelona.
Baschkiren, Bashkirs.
Bass Strasse, Bass's Strait.
Bassistis, Bashnia.
Baumwolle, Cotton.
Baumwolle u. Reis, Cotton and Rice.
Bayrische Alpen, Bavarian Alps.
Bayrisches Hochland, Bavarian Highlands.
Behrings Meer, Behring's Strait.
Behrings Meer od. Meer von Kamtschatka, Behring's Strait or Kamtschatkian Sea.
Belgien, Belgium.
Belice, Belici River.
Belochrobaten, Belochrobati (Slavonian tribe).
Belzoi See, Lake Belzoi.
Berenike, Bengazi.
Berg Andros, Mount Andros.
Berkley Sund, Berkeley Sound.
Bermudas od. Sommer I., Bermudas or Somers Islands.
Berner Alpen, Bernese Alps.
Bernstein Küste, Amber Coast.
Bessarabien, Bessarabia.
Bieler S., Lake of Biel.
Bjelos See, Lake Biellos.

Biled-ul-gerid, od. Dattelland, Biled-ul-gerid, or Land of Dates.
Biscayscher Meerbusen, Bay of Biscay.
Bithynien, Bithynium.
Blaue Bge., Blue Mountains.
Bodensee, Lake of Constance.
Böhmische Höhe, Bohemian Highlands.
Böhmischer Kessel, Bohemian Basin.
Bogen Indianer, Strongbow Indians (tribe of the Chippeways).
Bolzoi, oder Grosser See, Bolzoi or Large Lake.
Boreas (Nord), North Wind.
Borysthenes, Pripet River.
Borysthenes (Danapris), Dniepr River.
Bosnien, Bosna.
Bostra, Boszra.
Bothnischer Busen, Gulf of Botnia.
Bracara, Braga.
Brasilien, Brazil.
Brasilische Gebirge, Brazil Mountains.
Brasilische Strömung, Brazil Current.
Brasilisches Guyana, Brazil Guyana.
Braunschweig, Brunswick.
Brede Bugt, Bay of Brede.
Brienzer S., Lake of Brienz.
Brigantium, Briançon.
Britannien, Gr. Britain.
Britisches Guyana, British Guyana.
Brivates Haf, Bay of Brest.
Brüssel, Brussels.
Brundisium, Brindisi.
Brundusium, Brindisi.
Bucephala, Ihylum.
Bucharest, Bukarest.
Bucharien, Bokhara.
Buchweitzen, Buckwheat.
Bucinarische In. Buccinarian Islands.
Bulgaren, Bulgari (tribe on the lower Danube).
Burdigala, Bordeaux.
Burgunder, Burgundians.
Busen von Bengalien, Bay of Bengal.
Busen von Cadix, Bay of Cadiz.
Busen Carpentaria, Bay of Carpentaria.
Busen v. Danzig, Bay of Dantzig.
Busen von Lepanto oder von Korinth, Gulf of Lepanto or of Corinth.
Busen v. Lion, Gulf of Lyons.
Busen v. Lübeck, Bay of Lubeck.
Busen von Panama, Bay of Panama.
Busen von Taranto, Gulf of Taranto.
Busen von Tehuantepec, Gulf of Tehuantepec.
Busen von Triest, Gulf of Trieste.
Busen von Venedig, Bay of Venice.
Byblos, Djebail.
Byzacium, Tunis.
Byzant., Constantinople.

C. d. guten Hoffnung, Cape of Good Hope.
C. Horner Strömung, Cape Horn Current.
Cabillonus, Chalons.
Cæsar Augusta, Saragossa.
Cætobriga, Setobal.
Cajeta, Gaeta.
Caledonien, Caledonia.
Caledonischer Canal, Caledonian Canal.
Calvadosfelsen, Calvados Rocks.
Canal oder La Manche, the British Channel.
Canal u. Strömung v. Mozambique, Channel and current of Mozambique.
Canal von Yucatan, Channel of Yucatan.
Canarische Inseln, Canary Islands.
Candriaces, Nugor River.
Canopus, Aboukir.
Cantabrisches Geb. 600 *t.*, Santillanos Mountains 600 toises.
Cantal G., Cantal Mountains.
Cap Strom, Cape current.
Cap u. Ins. Breton, Cape and Island of Breton.
Cappadocien, Cappadocia.
Capsa, Wataras.
Capstadt, Cape Town.
Cuperdische Inseln, Cape Verde Islands.
Caraibisches Meer, Caribbean Sea.
Caralis, Cagliari.
Carenisches Gebirg, Sutherland Highlands.
Carmania, Kerman.
Carpathus, Scarpanto.
Carteja, Ocana.
Carthaginiensis Sinus, Gulf of Tunis.
Carthago, Carthage.
Carthago nova, Cartagena.
Casp. Engpässe, Caspian or Caucasian passes.
Caspisches Meer, Caspian Sea.
Caspisch. See liegt 33 t. unter d. Niveau d. Oceans, Caspian Sea, lies 33 toises lower than the level of the ocean.
Caspische See, Caspian Sea.
Cassiterides Ins., Scilly Islands.
Catalonien, Catalonia.

Celænæ, Dingla.
Cerasus, Keresoun.
Cevennen, Cevennes Mountains.
Chalifat der Abassiden, Caliphate of the Abassides.
Charolais Geb. Charolles Mountains.
Chemnis, Ekhmin.
Cherson, Kherson.
Chersonesus, Cape Razatin.
Cheviot Gebirge, Cheviot Hills.
Chile, Chili.
China Wälder, Bathbark Forests.
Chinesisches Meer, Chinese Sea.
Chios, Scio.
Choco Kette, Choco Mountain Chain.
Chorasmia See, Lake Kharasm.
Chorasmii, Kharasm.
Churhessen, Electoral Hesse.
Cibalis, Palanha.
Cilicia, Itshili ; *Die Cilicischen Thore*, the Passes of Itshili.
Cimbrische Halb I., Cimbrian Peninsula (Jutland).
Clearwater See, Clearwater Lake.
Cnossus, Macritichos.
Colchis, Mingrelia.
Colchischer G., Gulf of Mingrelia.
Colonia, Cologne.
Comana, Bostan.
Comer S., Lake of Como.
Comum, Como.
Conimbriga, Coimbra.
Constantinopel, Constantinople.
Constantinopolis, Constantinople.
Constanz, Constance.
Cooks Strasse, Cook's Strait.
Cophas, Guadel.
Cophes, Ghizni River.
Coptos, Ghouft.
Corcyra, Corfu.
Cordofan, Kordofan.
Corduba, Cordova.
Corps unter Hephæstion, Corps under Hephæstion.
Croatien, Croatia.
Croatische Militair Grenze, Croatian military frontier.
Curene, Kuren.
Curland, Courland.
Cydonia, Canea.
Cynopolis, Nesle Sheik Hassan.
Cypern, Cyprus.
Cyrene, West Barca.
Cyropolis, Enzellee.
Cyrus, Politica.
Cythere, Citria.
Cyzicus, Kyzik.

Dacia, Hungary and Transylvania.
Daenemark, Denmark.
Dakien, Dacia (Hungary).
Dalmatien, Dalmatia.
Dampfschiffe von Triest der Œstn. Lloyd Ges., Steamers of the Austrian Lloyd Company from Trieste.
Dänen, Danes.
Danubius, Danube River.
Danzig, Dantzig.
Daphne, Daia.
Dardanellen Schlösser, Palaces at the Dardanelles.
Dardanellen Str., Dardanelles.
Darnis, Derna.
Das Alpen Gebirge, the Alps.
Das Po Thal, the Po Valley.
Daurisches Alpenland, the Da Oural Alps (branch of the Oural Mountains).
Davis Strasse, Davis's Strait.
Delphi, Castri.
Dembo Hochland, Dembo Highlands.
D'Entrecasteaux Spitze, Point d'Entrecasteaux.
Der Normannen Reiche, the Norman Empires.
Der Spiegel des todten Meeres liegt 220 t. tiefer als der Ocean, the surface of the Dead Sea lies 220 toises below the level of the ocean.
Der Wash, the Wash.
Dergh See, Lake Derg.
Dertosa, Tortosa.
Deutsche Meilen 15 auf den Grad, German miles 15 to the degree.
Deutsche unter Kaiser Friedrich II., Germans under Emperor Frederick II.
Deutsches Kaiserreich, German Empire.
Deva, Ayas.
Die Aleuten od. Catharinas Archipel, the Aleutian Islands or Catharine's Archipelago.
Die Aleutischen Inseln, the Aleutian Islands.
Die Azoren, the Azores.
Die bekannte Welt des Alterthums, the world known to the Ancients.
Die Carolinen, the Caroline Islands.

Die 3 Oder Mündn., the three mouths of the Oder.

Die Eols Grotten, the Grottoes of Æolus.

Die grosse osteuropäische Ebene in welcher kein Punkt die Höhe von 180 t. erreicht, the large East-European plain, in which no point reaches the height of 180 toises.

Die Nord See oder das deutsche Meer, the North Sea or the German Sea.

Die Ostsee, oder das Baltische Meer, the Baltic.

Die Philippinen, the Philippine Islands.

Die Schweiz, Switzerland.

Die sieben Kuhfirsten, the Seven Cowridges.

Diemtiger Th., Diemtig Valley.

Dinarisches Alpen Gebirg, Dinarian Alps (on the lower Danube).

Dio Adelphi (Die 2 Brüder), Dio Adelphi (The Two Brothers).

Dioscorides I., Island of Socotra.

Dioscurias, Iskuria.

District diesseits der Donau, District north of the Danube.

District diesseits der Theiss, District west of the Theiss.

District jenseits der Donau, District beyond the Danube.

District jenseits der Theiss, District beyond (east of) the Theiss.

Dobrudscher, Dobrodje.

Donau, Danube.

Donaumündungen, Mouths of the Danube.

Donauwörth, Donauwerth.

Donische Kosaken, Cossacks of the Don.

Dora Baltea, Doria Baltea River.

Drapsaea, Bamian.

Drontheim, Trondheim.

Dschebil el Kamar od. Mond Geb., Gebel Komri, or Mountains of the Moon.

Düna, Dvina River.

Dünkirchen, Dunkirk.

Durius, Douro River.

Durovernum, Canterbury.

Eblana, Dublin.

Eboracum, York.

Ebro Mündung, Mouth of the Ebro.

Ebusus, Iviza.

Eisenbahnen, Railroads.

Eisenbahnkarte von Mitteleuropa, Railroad chart of Central Europe.

Eismeer, Arctic Ocean.

Eisstarre Sand u. Morast Fläche, Frozen Sand and Swamp Plain.

Elusa, Eauze.

Emerita Aug., Merida.

Emirat v. Cordova, Emirate of Cordova.

Enara See, Lake Enara.

Engländer unter Richard Löwenherz, the English under Richard Cœur de Lion.

Engl. Colonien am Schwanflusse, K. Georg's Sund und N. S. Wales, English Colonies on Swan River, King George's Sound, and New South Wales.

Englische Meilen 69.$\frac{22}{100}$ auf den Grad, English miles, 69.$\frac{22}{100}$ to the degree.

Engpass v. Kaipha, Pass of Kaipha.

Ephesus, Ayasaluk.

Epidaurus, Ragusa Vecchia.

Epirus, Albania.

Eregli, Erekli.

Erklärung der Zahlen, Explanation of the figures.

Erne See, Erne Loch.

Erymanthus, Mount Olonos.

Eskimos, Esquimaux.

Esthland, Esthonia.

Euböa, Negropont.

Euphrat, Euphrates.

Europa vor der Französischen Revolution, Europe before the French Revolution.

Europa zur Zeit der Kreuzzüge, Europe during the Crusades.

Europa zur Zeit Karls des Grossen, Europe at the time of Charlemagne.

Europäisch Sarmatien, European Sarmatia.

Europäische Besitzungen in Nord Guinea, European possessions in North Guinea.

Europäisches Russland, European Russia.

Europäisches Scythien, European Scythia.

Fadejewski, Fadevskoi.

Fær Œer, Faro Islands.

Falklands Ins., Falkland Islands.

Falsche Bai, Bay of Falso.

Faltschi, Faltsi.

Fan Œ., Fano I.

Favonius (West), West Wind (Zephyr).

Feuerland, Terra del Fuego.

Finnischer Busen, Gulf of Finland.

Fischereien von Agoutinitza, Fisheries of Agoutinitza.

Fittre See, Bahr Fittre.

Flachs u. Hanf, Flax and Hemp.

Flandern, Flanders.

Flavia Cäsariensis, Central England.

Flaviobriga, Bilbao.

Flavionavia, Laviana.

Flevus, Flevo, Zuyder Zee.

Florentia, Florence.

Florenz, Florence.

Franken, Franconia.

Frankfurt, Frankfort.

Fränkisches Italien, Frankish Italy.

Fränkisches Plateau, Franconian plateau.

Frankreich, France.

Französ. Guyana, French Guyana.

Französische Lieues 25 auf den Grad, French leagues 25 to the degree.

Franzosen unter Philipp August, The French under Philip Augustus.

Franzosen unter Ludwig IX., The French under Louis IX.

Freiburg, Freeburg.

Freie Indianer, Free Indians.

Freundschafts oder Tonga In., Friendly or Tonga Islands.

Friedens Fl., Peace River.

Frobischer Str., Frobisher's Strait.

Fuchs Ins., Fox Islands.

Fünen, Fyen.

Fuglæ, Bird Island.

Fürstm. Benevent, Principality of Benevento.

Fürstenthum Neuenburg, Principality of Neuenburg.

Gabæ, Chavos.

Gades, Cadiz.

Gaditanum, Gibraltar.

Galætia, Anadolia.

Galicien, Galicia.

Galizien, Galicia.

Gallien, Gallia (France).

Gallische Wegestunden wovon 50 auf den Grad, Gallic miles 50 to the degree.

Gangischer oder Indischer Golf, Bay of Bengal.

Garamantes, Fezzaneers and Tibboo (tribe).

Garda See, Lake of Garda.

Gaugamela, Kamalis.

Gaulos, Island of Goza.

Geb. v. Granada, Granada Mountains.

Gebirge von Auvergne, Mountains of Auvergne.

Gedros, Mekran.

Gelbes Meer, Yellow Sea.

Genf, Geneva.

Genfer See, Lake of Geneva.

Gent, Ghent.

Genua, Genoa.

Geographen B., Geographer's Bay.

Geogr. Meilen 15 auf den Grad, Geographical miles 15 to the degree.

Gepiden, Gepidæ (tribe).

Germanen, Germans.

Germanien, Germany.

Germanische Meer, North Sea.

Germanische Tiefebene, German Low Plain.

Gerste, Barley.

Gerste, Hafer, Roggen, Barley, Oats, Rye.

Gerste, Roggen, Kartoffeln und Buchweitzen, Barley, Rye, Potatoes, and Buckwheat.

Gesellschafts In., Society Islands.

Gesoriacum, Boulogne.

Geten, Getæ (tribe).

Gletscher, Glacier.

Glückliches Arabien, Arabia Felix.

Gogana, Congoon.

Göksschai See, Lake Gokshai.

Goldener Chersonesus, Golden Khersonesus (Malaya).

Gordium, Sarilar.

Gorsynia, Atchicola.

Gothen, Goths.

Gr. Bären See, Great Bear Lake.

Gr. Minsh oder Caledonisches Meer, Great Minsh or Caledonian Sea.

Gr. Sclaven S., Great Slave Lake.

Grampian Gebirge, Grampian Mountains.

Graubündner Alpen, Grison Alps.

Griechenland, Greece.

Griechisches Italien, Greek Italy.

Grönland, Greenland.

Gross Britannien und Ireland, Great Britain and Ireland.

Gross Phrygia, Phrygia Major.

Gross Russland, Great Russia.

Grosse Antillen, the larger Antilles (West India Islands).

Grosse Eskimos, Great Esquimaux.

Grosser Atlas, Mount Atlas.

Grosser oder Stiller Ocean, Pacific Ocean.

Grossherz. Hessen, Grand Duchy of Hesse.

Grüne Berge, Green Mountains.

Grünes Vorgebirge, Cape Verde.

Gürtel des Getreides, Zone of the grains.

Gürtel ohne Cultur, Zone without cultivation.

Guräus, Kamah River.

H. I. or Halbinsel stands for "Peninsula" before the respective names.

Haag, the Hague.

Habesch, Habesh.

Hadrianopolis, Adrianople.

Hæmus, Balkan Mountains.

Haf. v. or Hafen von stands for "Port of" before the respective names.

Hafer, Oats.

Hafer u. Gerste, Oats and Barley.

Hafer u. Weitzen, Oats and Wheat.

Halbinsel Methana, Peninsula of Dara (Methana).

Halicarnassus, Boodroom.

Haliez oder Galizien, Galicia.

Han Hai (Südl. Meer), South Sea.

Harz Gb., Harz Mountains.

Hasen Ind., Hare Indians.

Haupt Æquatorial Strömung, Principal equatorial current.

Hauptstadt, Capital.

Hebräische Stadien wovon 750 a. d. Gr., Hebrew stadia 750 to the degree.

Hebriden oder Western Inseln, Hebrides or Western Islands.

Hecatompylos, Danghan.

Hedschas, Hedjas.

Heiliges Vgb., Promontorium Sacrum.

Heliopolis, Baalbec.

Hellas, Greece.

Hellespontus, Dardanelles.

Helsingör, Elsinore.

Heniochi, Tribe in Armenia.

Hermopolis, Eshmounein.

Hermunduren, Hermunduri (tribe in central Germany).

Herodots Erdtafel, Herodotus's Map of the World.

Heruler, Heruli (tribe in North Germany).

Herzogl. Sächsische Länder, Saxon Duchies.

Herzogthum, Duchy.

Hibernien, Hibernia.

Hinter Rhein, Hind Rhine (one of the rivulets tributary to the Rhine).

Hippo Regius, Bona.

Hispalis, Seville.

Hispanien, Spain.

Hoch Alp, High Alp.

Hoch Sudan, Soudah Mountains.

Hochland von Africa, Highlands of Africa.

Hohe Tatarei, Tartar Highlands.

Hoher Atlas, Mount Atlas.

Hügelgruppe v. Sandomir, Group of Hills of Sandomir.

Hunds Ribben Ind, Dogrib Indians.

Hunigaren oder Ungrier, Hungarians.

Hydraotes, Ravee River.

Hypanis, Kuban River.

Hyphasis, Beyah River.

Hyrcania, Gyrgaun.

Hyrkanisch. Meer, Caspian Sea.

I., Ia., Ins., or Insel stands for "Island" before the respective names.

I. Helgoland, Island of Heligoland.

I. Kangurah, Kangaroo Island.

I. u. Stadt Cayenne, Island and Town of Cayenne.

Jacobs Thal, Jacob's Valley.

Jadera, Zarah.

Japanisches Meer, Sea of Japan.

Jasygien, Jassygia.

Jaxartes, Sihon River.

Jazygen (Sarmaten), Sarmatians.

Ibenes, Ebro River.

Iberia, Georgia.

Ichthyophagen, Fish-eaters.

Iconium, Konia.

Jenseits d. Ganges, Beyond the Ganges.

Jenseits d. Imaus, Beyond the Altai.

Jernis, Dunkerrin.

Illyricum, Illyria.

Illyrien, Illyria.

Im Sommer 15°, In the summer 66 degrees F.

Im Winter 5°, In the winter 43 degrees F.

Imandra See, Lake Imandra.

Imaus Geb., Altai Mountains.

Indischer Ocean, Indian Ocean.

Indsche Burun, Cape Indjeh.

Indus Mündn., Mouths of the Indus.

Ins. unter d. Winde, Caribbean Islands.

Ins. d. günen Vorgebirges, Cape Verde Islands

Jomanes, Jumna River.

Jonische Inseln, Ionian Islands.

Joppe, Yaffa.
Joux See, Lake Joux.
Ipsus, Ipsilihissar.
Irgis, Irghiz River.
Irische See, Irish Sea.
Irland, Ireland.
Irtisch, Irtish River.
Is, Hit.
Isca, Exe River.
Island, Iceland.
Issedones, Mongolian tribe.
Ister (Donau), Danube.
Ister Mündn., Mouths of the Danube.
Italien, Italy.
Jülich, Juliers.
Jüten, Jutlanders.
Juliobriga, Reynosa.
Julische Alpen, Carnic or Julian Alps.
Jura Geb., Jura Mountains.
Jura Sund, Jura Sound.
Juvavia, Saltzburg.

K. Charlotte S., Queen Charlotte's Sound.
Kärnthen, Carinthia.
Kaiser Canal, Emperor's Canal.
Kaiserthum Œsterreich, Empire of Austria.
Kalmüken, Calmucks.
Kamische Bulgaren, Kama Bulgarians.
Kanäle, Canals.
Kanal von Bristol, Bristol Channel.
Kaptschak, Cabjak (tribe in Bokhara).
Karafta oder Sachalin, Caraphta or Sachalin.
Karazubazar, Kara Soo.
Karchedon, Carthage.
Karischer B., Bay of Caria.
Karmanien, Kerman.
Karolinen, Caroline Islands.
Karpathen 2000 t. mittl. Höhe, Carpathian Mountains 2000 toises mean height.
Karpathen Geb., Carpathian Mountains.
Karpathisches Waldgebirge, Carpathian Forest.
Kartagena, Cartagena.
Karthago, Carthage.
Kartoffeln u. Hafer, Potatoes and Oats.
Kartoffeln u. Buchweitzen, Potatoes and Buckwheat.
Kaspisches Meer, Caspian Sea.
Kattegat, Cattegat.
Kaukasien, Caucasia.
Kaukasus Gebirge, Caucasian Mountains.
Kaukasische Steppe, Caucasian Steppes.
Keine Bäume ab. Graswuchs, No trees but grass.
Kelten, Celts.
Kemi See, Lake Kemin.
Kgn. Charlotte I., Queen Charlotte's Island.
Kimbrischer Cherson, Cimbrian Chersonesus (Jutland).
Kjölen Gebirge, Koelen Mountains.
Kirchenstaat, Papal States.
Kirgisen Horde, Kirghis Horde.
Kirghisen Steppe, Kirghis Steppes.
Kizil Ermak, Kizil Irmak River.
Kl. Antillen, Little Antilles (Caribbean Islands).
Kl. Karpathen, Little Carpathians.
Kl. Kumanien, Kis Kunsag.
Klein Phrygia, Phrygia Minor.
Klein Russland, Little Russia (Russian Province).
Kleinasien, Asia Minor.
Kleine Kirgisen Horde, Little Kirghis Horde.
Koblenz, Coblentz.
Köln, Cologne.
Kön. Georg Sund, King George's Sound.
König. Georg's I., King George's Islands.
Königin Charlotte Sund, Queen Charlotte's Sound.
Königreich stands for "kingdom" before the respective names.
Konäguen, Tribe of Esquimaux.
Kong Gebirge, Mountains of Kong.
Kopenhagen, Copenhagen.
Kosaken, Cossacks.
Krakau, Cracow.
Krym, Crimea.
Kuba, Cuba.
Kupfer Ind., Copper Indians.

L. I. Sund, Long Island Sound.
Ladoga See, Lake Ladoga.
Lakeneig, Lakeneigh.
Laminium, Alambra.
Lamose, Lamusa River.
Lampsacus, Lamsaki.
Lanai, Tribe in North Germany.
Lancerote, Lancerota Island.
Land der Finnen, Land of the Finns.
Land der kleinen Eskimos, Land of the dwarf Esquimaux.
Larice, Lack.
Lauriacum, Lorch.
Lausitzer Gebirg, Lusatian Mountains.

Leba See, Lake Leba.
Leman S., Lake Leman.
Leptis, Lebida.
Lerdalsöer, Lerdals Islands.
Lesbos, Mytilene.
Lessöewerk, Lessoe forge.
Leucas, Amaxiki.
Leuce, Island of Adasi.
Ljœchen, Bohemians.
Libyen, Africa.
Libysche Wüste, Libyan Desert.
Lieukieu In., Loo Choo Islands.
Ligeris, Loire River.
Liguria, Genoa.
Ligurisches Meer, Gulf of Genoa.
Likeio In., Loo Choo Islands.
Lilybœum, Boe.
Lindum, Lincoln.
Liptauer Alp, Liptau Alps.
Lissus, Allessio.
Lithauer, Lithuania.
Litus Saxonum, Coast of Sussex.
Litwanen, Lithuania.
Livadien, Livadia.
Liviner Thal, Livin Valley.
Livland, Livonia.
Livorno, Leghorn.
Lixus, Luccos River.
Loja, Loxa.
Lombardei, Lombardy.
Lomond S., Lake Lomond.
Londinum, London.
Longobarden, Longobardi (Lombards).
Lucentum, Alicante.
Luceria, Lucera.
Lüneburger Heide, Luneburg Heath.
Lüttich, Liège.
Lugdunensis, North West France.
Lugdunum, Leyden.
Lugovallum, Carlisle.
Lugumkloster, Lugum Convent.
Lulea See, Lake Lulea.
Lumnitz B., Mount Lomnitz.
Lusitania, Portugal.
Lutitschen, Luititsi or Wilzi (Tribe in North Germany).
Luzern, Lucerne.
Lycaonia, N. W. Karamania.
Lyon, Lyons.
Lystra, Illisera.

Maas, Meuse River.
Maasstäbe, Scales.
Macedonien, Macedonia.
Mackenzie In., Mackenzie's Islands.
Macquarie In., Macquarie's Island.
Madgyaren, Magyars.
Mähren, Moravia.
Mährische Höhe, Moravian Highlands.
Mælar See, Lake Mælar.
Maeotis See, Sea of Azov.
Magelhaens Strasse, Straits of Magallan.
Mahadia, Mahedia.
Mahrah, Mahran.
Mailand, Milan.
Mainz, Mayence, Maynz.
Mais und Weitzen, Indian Corn and **Wheat**.
Makarjew, Makariv.
Mal Ström, Malstrom.
Malaca, Malacca.
Malmö, Malmo.
Malmysch, Malmish.
Malouinen, Falkland Islands.
Mandeln, Almonds.
Mandschurei, Manchooria.
Manytsch, Manich River.
Maraniten, Maranites, tribe in Arabia Felix.
Marcomannen, Marcomanni, tribe in S. E. Germany.
Mare Adriaticum, Adriatic Sea.
Mare Caspium, Caspian Sea.
Mare Erythrœum (Indisches Meer), Indian Ocean.
Mare Hyrcanum oder Casplum, Caspian Sea.
Mare Internum (Mittelländisches Meer), Mediterranean Sea.
Marea, El Khreit.
Margaret In., Margaret's Island.
Margus, Murghab River.
Marianen od. Ladronen, Marian Islands.
Marinestunden 25 auf den Grad, Marine leagues 25 to the degree.
Marisus, Maros River.
Marmara Meer, Sea of Marmora.
Marschall Inseln, Mulgrave Islands.
Marseille, Marseilles.
Martyropolis, Meia Farekin.
Mascarenen Inseln, Mascarenhas Islands (Mauritius, Bourbon, &c.).
Massaga, Massa.

Massilia, Marseilles.
Mater, Matter.
Mauritania, Algiers.
Mauritanien, Algiers.
Maxima Cœsariensis, Northern England.
Mb. v. Issus (Sinus Issilicus), Bay of Iskenderoon.
Meder, Medes (nation).
Mediolanum, Milan.
Medus, Abkuren River.
Meer Alpen, Maritime Alps.
Meer von Ochotsh, Sea of Okotsk.
Meer von Tarrakai, Gulf of Tartary.
Meerb. v. Californien, Gulf of California.
Meerb. v. Sues, Gulf of Suez.
Meerbusen von Mexico, Gulf of Mexico.
Meiningen, Meinungen.
Melgig Sumpf, Melgig Swamp.
Melitene, Malatia.
Memel od. Niemen, Meman River.
Memel Niederung, Tilsit Lowlands.
Memnis, Korkor Baba.
Memphis, Mangel Mousa, or Mit Raheni.
Meninx, Jerba Island.
Mergui In., Mergue Archipelago.
Meroe, Gibbainy.
Mesagna, Mesagne.
Mesembria, Missivri.
Mesopotamia, Al Gezira.
Messana, Messina.
Mettis, Metz.
Mexicanische Küstenströmung, Mexican Coast Current.
Miletus, Palatia.
Militär Colonien, Military Colonies.
Militair Grenze, Military Boundary.
Minius, Minho River.
Miö See, Lake Miœ.
Mioritz See, Lake Mioritz.
Mississippi Mündungen, Mouths of the Mississippi.
Mittelländisches Meer, Mediterranean Sea.
Mittlere Kirgisen Horde, Middle Kirghis Horde.
Mittlere Temperatur nach Celsius, Mean temperature according to Celsius.
Mittlere Temperatur nach Reaumur, Mean temperature according to Reaumur.
Mogontiacum, Mayntz.
Molukken, Molucca Islands.
Molukken Str., Molucca Passage.
Mond Gebirg, Mountains of the Moon.
Mongolei, Mongolia.
Monreale, Monreal.
Montagnes Noires, Black Mountains (Black Forest).
Mordwinen, Mordwines (tribe in Asiatic Russia).
Moreton C. u. B., Moreton Cape and Bay.
Moscha, Morebat.
Mosel, Moselle River.
Moskenasö, Mosken Island.
Moskau, Moscow.
Moskwa, Moskow.
Mosyneoci (tribe on the Black Sea).
Mozyr, Mozir.
Mühlhausen, Mulhouse.
München, Munich.
Mündung des Amazonen Stroms, Mouth of the Amazon River.
Mündung der Elbe, Mouth of the Elbe.
Mündung des Tajo, Mouth of the Tagus.
Murray Busen, Murray Firth.
Muthmassliche Grenze der den Alten bekannten Binnenländer von Afrika nach den Geographen Walkenaer und Gosselin, Probable boundary of the African inland known to the Ancients according to the geographers Walkenaer and Gosselin.
Mutina, Modena.

N. Schottl., North Scotland.
N. W. Ausflüsse des Æquatorial Stroms, Northwest termination of the Equatorial Current.
Nabathœer, Nabathæi (nation in Arabia).
Nadel Banck, Cape Agulhas.
Naissus, Nissa.
Namadus, Nerbuddah River.
Napeta, Mograt.
Narbona, Narbonne.
Narbonensis, Narbonne.
Nasamonen, Nasamones (tribe in West Barca).
Natal Küste, Natal Coast.
Nausa mit Hafer, Nausa, with port.
Nazareth Bank und Ins., Nazaret Bank and Island.
Neagh S., Lake Neagh.
Neapel (Neapolis), Naples.
Nelson Canal, Nelson Channel.
Nemausus, Nismes.
Nerbudda, Nerbuddah River.
Neu stands for "New" before the respective names.
Neu Californien, New California.

Neu Georgien, New Georgia.
Neu Helvetien, New Helvetia.
Neu Karthago, New Carthage.
Neu Scotia, Nova Scotia.
Neu Sibirien, New Siberia.
Neue Hebriden, New Hebrides.
Neue Saline, New Saltwork.
Neuenburg, Neufchatel.
Neuenburger S., Lake of Neufchatel.
Neustrien, Neustria (the part of France lying between the Meuse, Loire, and the Atlantic Ocean).
Nicasia, Island of Karos.
Nicobaren, Nicobar Islands.
Nicomedia, Izmid.
Nieder Canada, Lower Canada.
Nieder Ungarische Ebene, Lower Hungarian Plain.
Niederl. Guyana, Dutch Guyana.
Niederlande, Netherlands.
Niger, Niger River.
Nil, Nile River.
Nil Mündungen, Mouths of the Nile
Nilus, Nile River.
Nimes, Nismes.
Niphates Geb., Sepan Mountains.
Nizza, Nice.
Norba Cæsaria, Alcantara.
Nördlicher Oceanus, Arctic Ocean.
Nördlicher Polarkreis, Arctic Circle.
Nördlicher Wolga Rücken, Northern Volga Ridge.
Nördliches Eismeer, Arctic Ocean.
Nord stands for "North" before the respective names.
Nord Afrikanische Strömung, North African Current.
Nord Albinger, North Albingians (tribe in Holstein).
Nord Georgien, North Georgia.
Nord Georgien I., North Georgia Island.
Nord See, North Sea.
Noricum, Styria, Salzburg, &c.
Norische Alpen, Noric Alps.
Normanische Inseln, Normandy Islands (Guernsey, Jersey, Alderney, Sark).
Northlined S., Northlined Lake.
Norwegen, Norway.
Notium Vgb., Mizen Head.
Nuba See, Nuba Lake.
Nuba Sumpf, Nuba Swamp.
Nubier, Nubians (tribe).
Nubische Wüste, Nubian Desert.
Numidien, Numidia (East Algiers).
Nursa, Norcia.
Nymegen, Nimegue.

Obdorisches Gebirge, Obdorsk Mountains (Northern extremity of the Oural Ms).
Ober See, Lake Superior.
Obi, Oby Island.
Obotriten, Obotrites (Vandal tribe in North Germany).
Oceanus Atlanticus, Atlantic Ocean.
Oceanus Germanicus, North Sea.
Ochus See, mit dem Kaspisches Meere früher wahrscheinlich zusammenhängend, Ochus Sea (Aral Sea), probably formerly connected with the Caspian Sea.
Odessus, Odessa.
Odyssus, Odessa.
Œ. L. v. Ferro, East longitude from the Island of Ferro.
Œ. L. v. Paris, East longitude from Paris.
Œca, Tripoli.
Œlbäume, Olive trees.
Œsterreich, Austria.
Œsterreichische Alpen, Austrian Alps.
Œsterreichische Landestheile, Austrian dependencies.
Œstl. Gats, Eastern Ghauts.
Œstliche Länge von Ferro, East longitude from the Island of Ferro.
Œstliche Länge von Paris, East longitude from Paris
Offene B., Open Bay.
Olisibon (Olisipo), Lisbon.
Olite, Olitte.
Olivenza, Olivenca.
Olympia, Miraoea.
Olympische Stadien wovon 600 a. d. Grad, Olympic stadia, 600 to the degree.
Onega See, Onega Lake.
Ophiusa, Island of Formentera.
Orange od. Gariep, Orange or Gariep River.
Orangen, Oranges.
Orbelus, Mt. Gliubotin.
Orchoe, Bassora.
Oregon oder Felsen Gebirge, Rocky Mountains.
Oregon od. Columbia, Columbia River.

Orinoco Münd., Mouth of the Orinoco.
Orkaden, Orkney Islands.
Orscha, Orsha.
Orsowa, Orsova.
Ortles Sp., Ortler Spitz.
Ortospanum, Kandahar.
Osca, Huesca.
Osmanisches Asien, Ottoman Asia.
Osmanisches Reich, Ottoman Empire.
Ossa, Mount Kissovo.
Ossadiæ (tribe in India).
Ost stands for "East" before the respective names.
Ost Küste von Brasilien, East Coast of Brazil.
Ost Preussen, East Prussia.
Ost Pyrenäen, East Pyrenees.
Ost See, Baltic.
Ost Römisches Kaiserreich, East Roman Empire.
Ostphalen, Eastphalians (tribe of the Saxon nation).
Ostracine, Ras Straki.
Ostrogothen, Ostrogoths.
Othrys Gebirg, Othrys (Hellovo) Mountains.
Ottomaken, Ottomak Indians.
Oxus, Amoo River.
Oxyrynchus, Behenese.
Oxydraces, Oxydracæ (tribe in Moultan).
Ozark Gebirg, Ozark Mountains.

P. Gr. d. Getreides u. d. Zone d. Regens, Polar boundary of grain and of the zone of rain.
P. Gr. d. Weines u. d. europäisch. tropen. Getreides, Polar boundary of the grape vine and of European tropical grain.
Padua, Padova.
Padus, Po River.
Pæstum, Pesto.
Palästina, Palestine.
Palibothra (Palimbothra), Patna.
Palks Strasse, Palk's Straits.
Palmyra oder Tadmor, Palmyra or Tadmor.
Palus Mæotis, Sea of Azov.
Pamphylia, S. E. Anadolia.
Pandosia, Mendicino.
Pannonia, Hungary.
Pannonien, Hungary.
Panormus, Raphti.
Panticapæum, Kertch.
Paphlagonia, N. E. Anadolia.
Paphos, Baffa.
Parætonium, Al Bareton.
Parisii, nation in North France.
Paropanusus Geb., Hindoo Koosh.
Parthia, Province in Khorasan and N. E. Irak.
Parthiscus (Tibiscus), Theiss River.
Pasargadæ (Persepolis), Istakar.
Pastona, Pasten.
Patagonien, Patagonia.
Patagonische Kette, Patagonian Cordilleras.
Pax Julia, Beja.
Pella, Allahkilissia.
Pelopones, Morea.
Pelusium, Tineh.
Penninische Alpen, Pennine Alps.
Pentapolis, Chittagong.
Pentland Strasse, Pentland Firth.
Pergamus, Pergamo.
Pers. Golf, Gulf of Persia.
Persien, Persia.
Persische Parasangen, wov. 25 a. d. Gr., Persian Parasangs, 25 to the degree.
Persischer M. B., Gulf of Persia.
Peruanische Strömung, Peruvian Current.
Petschenegen, Petsheneqs (Tartar tribe).
Peucetia, Terra di Bari.
Peuciner, Peucini (tribe in Galicia, &c.).
Phanagoria, Tmutarakan.
Pharsalus, Pharsala.
Pharselis, Tekrova.
Phazania, Fezzan.
Philippi, Filibah.
Philippinen, Philippine Islands.
Philippopel, Philippopolis.
Phocæa, Fokies.
Phryger, Phrygians (nation in Anadolia).
Physikalische Karte von Europa (— Afrika, — Asien, — Nord America, — Süd Amerika), Physical map of Europe (— Africa, — Asia, — North America, — South America).
Pictavi (nation in Gallia Aquitania).
Picten, Picts (nation in Scotland).
Pielis See, Lake of Pielis.
Pindus Mn., Agrafa and Smocovo Mountains.
Pisidia, S. E. Anadolia.
Pithyusen (Pityusæ), Islands of Iviza, Formentera, &c.
Pityus, Soukoum.
Pitkarainen, Pitcairn's Island.
Plateau v. (or von) stands for "Plateau of" before the respective names.
Plateau von Ost Galizien, Plateau of East Galicia.

Plattkopf Indr., Flathead Indians.
Podolien, Podolia.
Polænen, Polænæ (Slavonic tribe).
Polargr. d. Bäume, Polar boundary of trees.
Polargr. d. Moose u. Beeren, Polar boundary of mosses and berries.
Polargr. d. Obstbaumes, Polar boundary of fruit trees.
Polargr. d. Œlbaumes, Polar boundary of the olive tree.
Polargr. d. Weinstocks, Polar boundary of the grape vine.
Polargrenze, Polar boundary.
Polargrenze d. Banane u. d. tropischen Getreides, Polar boundary of the banana and of the tropical grain.
Polargrenze des Getreides, Polar boundary of grain.
Polargrenze d. Palmen, Polar boundary of palm trees.
Polargrenze d. Weinstocks u. d. europäisch. trop. Getreides, Polar boundary of the grape vine and of the European tropical grain.
Polar Kreis, Arctic (or Antarctic) Circle.
Polen, Poland.
Polesiens Urwälder u. Sümpfe, Primitive forests and swamps of Polesia (now Minsk in Russia).
Pommern, Pomerania.
Pompelo, Pampeluna.
Pont. Eux. (Pontus Euxinus), Black Sea.
Pontinische In., Ponza Islands.
Pontus, N. E. Bulgaria.
Pontus Euxinus (Schwarzes Meer), Black Sea.
Porata, Pruth River.
Portland Sp., Portland Point.
Prag, Prague.
Prairien, Prairies.
Premnis, Cas. of Ibrim.
Pr. Holland, Prussian Holland (district in East Prussia).
Preussen, Prussia.
Preussische Landestheile, Prussian districts.
Preussische Höhe, Prussian Plateau.
Prophtasia (Prophthasia), Dookshak.
Propontis, Sea of Marmora.
Pskow, Pskov.
Psyllen, Psylli (tribe in N. Africa).
Ptolemäische Erdtafel, Map of the world according to Ptolemy.
Ptolemäische Stadien wovon 700 auf den Grad, Ptolemæan stadia 700 to the degree.
Pudosh, Pudog.
Pura, Pureg.
Purpur Ins., Purpureæ Insulæ (probably Salvage Islands).
Putea, Fuentes.
Putziger Wiek, Bay of Putzig.
Pyrenæi, Pyrenees.
Pyrenäen, Pyrenees.
Pyreneos Geb., Pyrenees.

Quaden, Quadi (nation in Hungary).
Quadra u. Vancouvers I., Vancouver's Island.
Querimbe, Querimba.

Rathenow, Rathenau.
Ratiaria, Arcer Palanka.
Rauhe Alp, Rauhe Alpe.
Rauraci, Tribe in Alsace.
Rch. d. Picten, Kingdom of the Picts.
Ree See, Lake Ree.
Regen Fluss, Rain River.
Regen S., Rain Lake.
Regenloses Gebiet, Rainless territory.
Regensburg, Ratisbon.
Reich der Aglabiten, Kingdom of the Aglabites (dynasty of Ibrahim ben Aglab).
Reich Alexanders des Grossen, Empire of Alexander the Great.
Reich der Bulgaren, Empire of the Bulgarians.
Reich der Chazaren, Empire of the Chazares (nation in East Russia).
Reich Karls d. Gr., Empire of Charlemagne.
Reich des Porus, Kingdom of Porus (in India).
Reich der Seleuciden, Kingdom of the Seleucidæ (dynasty of Seleucus).
Reich der Slaven, Empire of the Slavonians.
Reiche d. Angelsaxen, Anglo-Saxon Possessions.
Reiche d. Briten, Possessions of the Britons.
Reiche d. Dänen, Possessions of the Danes.
Reiche d. Scoten, Possessions of the Scots.
Reis und Kaffee, Rice and Coffee.
Reis und Mais, Rice and Indian Corn.
Republik Genua, Republic of Genoa.
Republik Venedig, Republic of Venice.
Reus, Reuss.
Reval, Revel.
Rha (Wolga), Rha (Volga).
Rhätische Alpen, Rhætian Alps.
Rhagæ, Rha.

Rhein, Rhine River.
Rhein Bayern, Rhenish Bavaria.
Rhegium, Reggio.
Rheims, Reims.
Rhenus, Rhine.
Rhoda, Rosas.
Rhodanus, Rhone River.
Rhodus, Rhodes.
Rhön Gb., Hohe Rhœne Mountains.
Rhoxolani, Rhoxolani (Sarmatian tribe).
Römisch Deutsches Kaiserreich, Romano-Germanic Empire.
Römische Meilen wovon 75 auf den Grad, Roman miles 75 to the degree.
Römisches Reich, Roman Empire.
Römisches Reich zur Zeit Constantins des Grossen, Roman Empire in the time of Constantine the Great.
Roggen, Gerste, Weitzen, Rye, Barley, Wheat.
Roggen u. Gerste, Rye and Barley.
Roggen und Weitzen, Rye and Wheat.
Rom, Rome.
Roma, Rome.
Rothes od. Erythräisches Meer, Red Sea.
Rothes Meer od. Arabischer Meerb, Red Sea.
Rotomagus, Rouen.
Rozolanen, Roxolani (Sarmatian tribe).
Rückkehr der Flotte unter Nearch, Return of the fleet under Nearchus.
Rücklaufende Strömung, Counter current.
Ruinen v. Babylon, Ruins of Babylon.
Ruinen von Carthago, Ruins of Carthage.
Ruinen v. Palmyra, Ruins of Palmyra.
Ruinen v. Susa, Ruins of Susa.
Rumanier, Rumini (tribe in Bulgaria, Moldavia, and Moravia).
Rusadir, Melilla.
Rusicada, Stora.
Ruspæ, Sbea.
Russische Werste 104.3 auf den Grad, Russian Wersts 104.3 to the degree.
Russische America, Russian America.
Russlands beste Kornfelder, Russia's best grainfields.
Rusucurrum, Koleah.

Saas Thal, Saas Valley.
Sabier, Sabians (St. John the Baptist's disciples; sect in Persia).
Sachalites Golf, Bay of Seger.
Sachsen, Saxony.
Sächsische Schweiz, Saxonian Switzerland.
Saguntum, Murviedro.
Saima S., Lake Saim.
Saker, Sakr.
Salamis, Coulouri.
Salmantica, Salamanca.
Salomons Ins., Solomon Islands.
Saloniki, Salonica.
Salz Seen, Salt Lakes.
Salz Wüste, Salt Desert.
Sambus, Chumbul River.
Samojeden, Samoyedes.
Samoa oder Schiffer In., Navigators' Islands.
Samosate, Samisat.
Samsun, Samsoun.
Sandw. Cobi od. Hanhai, Desert of Cobi.
Sand Wüste, Sandy Desert.
Sangarius, Sakariah River.
Sarazenen, Saracens or Moors.
Sardes, Sart.
Sardica, Sophia.
Sardinien, Sardinia.
Sariphi Geb., Shar Mountains.
Sarmatæ, Sarmatians.
Sarmatien, Sarmatia.
Sarmatische Tiefebene, Sarmatian Lowland (East Prussia, Poland, and part of Russia).
Sarmatisches Meer, Sarmatian Sea (part of the Baltic).
Sarnia, Island of Guernsey.
Satala, Shaygran.
Sauromaten, Sarmatians.
Saxen, Saxony (Saxonians, Saxons).
Scandinavisches Meer, Scandinavian Sea.
Schetland In., Shetland Islands.
Schlangen Indr., Snake Indians.
Schlesien, Silesia.
Schloss v. Romelli, Romelli Castle.
Schnee Alp, Snowy Alps.
Schotland, Scotland.
Schwäbische Alp, Suabian Mountains.
Schwarzes Meer 52 t. tief, Black Sea 52 toises deep.
Schwarzw. (ald), Black Forest.
Schweden, Sweden.
Schweden, Norwegen und Dänemark, Sweden, Norway, and Denmark.
Schwedische Landestheile, Swedish districts.
Schweiz, Switzerland.

Sclaven K. (üste), Slave Coast.
Scodra, Scutari.
Scordisci, tribe in Slavonia.
Scythopolis, Bysan.
Scupi, Uskup.
Scylacium, Squillace.
See, Sea or Lake.
See Alpen, Maritime Alps.
See Alpen von Californien, Maritime Alps of California.
See Alpen der Nord West Küste, Maritime Alps of the N. W. Coast.
See Arsissa, Lake Van.
See Küsten Kette v. Venezuela, Sea coast mountain chain of Venezuela.
See Likari, Lake Likaris.
Seehunds B., Seal's or Shark's Bay.
Seeland, Zealand.
Seemeilen 20 auf den Grad, Sea miles 20 to the degree.
Segobriga, Segorbe.
Seliger S., Lake Seligero.
Selinus, Vostizza River.
Senegambien, Senegambia.
Senogallia (Lugdunensis quarta), Isle of France and Champagne.
Senus, Shannon River.
Septentrio (Nord), North.
Septimanen, Septimani (tribe in Languedoc).
Serbien, Servia.
Sesamus, Amasserah.
Setuval, Setubal.
Sevennen, Cevennes Mountains.
Seychellen Ins., Seychelle Islands.
Shetland Inseln, Shetland Islands.
Shin See, Shin Lake.
Sicilia, Sicily.
Sidodona, Shenaas.
Sidon, Sayda.
Siebenbürgen, Transylvania.
Siebenbürgisches Plateau, Plateau of Transylvania.
Siena, Sienna.
Siga, Takumbreet.
Signia, Segni.
Sil, Sile River.
Simferopol, Taurida.
Simmen Thal, Simm Valley.
Singaglia, Sinigaglia.
Singara, Sinjar.
Singidunum, Belgrade.
Siniope, Sinub.
Sinus Arabicus, Red Sea.
Sirmium, Alt Schabacz.
Siscia, Sziszek.
Sitacus, Sita Rhegian River.
Sitife, Seteef.
Skagerak, Skager Rack.
Skagestrandsbugt u. Handelsted, Skager Beach Bay and Commercial Town.
Skandien (Scandia), Sweden.
Skythen, Scythians (nation).
Skythini (Scythini), probably Saracens in Armenia.
Slaven, Slavonians.
Slavonische Militair Grenze, Slavonian military frontier.
Slowenen, Wends (Slavonic nation).
Sogdiana, Great Bukaria.
Sogdianien (Sogdiana), Great Bukaria.
Solanus (Ost), East.
Soledad od. Ost I., Soledad or Eastern Island (Falkland Islands).
Soli, Mezetlu.
Soraben, Sorbi (Slavonic tribe).
Span. Mark, Spanish mark (modern Catalonia, Navarre, and part of Arragonia).
Spanien, Spain.
Speier, Speyer.
Spoletum, Spoleto.
St. Georgs Kanal, St. George's Channel.
St. Johann, St. John.
Staaten der Mexicanischen Union, States of the Mexican Union.
Staaten der Nordamerikanischen Union, States of the North American Union.
Staatenland, Staten Island (S. A.).
Stadt der Getæ, City of the Getæ.
Stalaktiden Grotte, Stalactite Grotto.
Steyermark, Styria.
Str. v. (Strasse von) stands for "Straits of" before the respective names.
Strabo's Erdtafel, Map of the World according to Strabo.
Strasse v. Calais, the British Channel.
Strom und Gebirgs-System von Mitteleuropa, River and Mountain System of Central Europe.
Südamerika, South America.
Süd Atlantische Strömung, South Atlantic Current.

Süd Cap, South Cape.
Süd Georgien, South Georgia.
Südl. Continent, Southern Continent.
Südl. Grenze des Weinstocks, Southern boundary of the grape vine.
Südliche Verbindungs Strömung, Southern Connecting Current.
Südlicher Polarkreis, Antarctic Circle.
Süd oder Neu Georgien, South or New Georgia.
Süd Schetland, New South Shetland.
Süd West, South West.
Sümpfe in gleicher Höhe m. d. Ocean, Swamps on a level with the ocean.
Sumpf, Swamp.
Sund, Sound.
Sunda See, Sea of Sunda.
Sunda Strasse, Straits of Sunda.
Susiana, Khuzistan and Louristan.
Swilly See, Lake Swilly.
Sybaris, Cochyle River.
Syracusa, Syracuse.
Syrdaria, Sir River.
Syrien, Syria.
Syrisch Arabische Wüste, Syro-Arabian Desert.
Syrische Wüste, Syrian Desert.
Syrtes, Gulf of Sidra.
Syrtika (Seli or Psylli), in Tripolis.

Tabor, Mt. Tor.
Tabraca, Tabarca.
Tacape, Cabes.
Tafelland von Armenien 250 t., Armenian Plateau 250 toises.
Tafelland von Iran 650 t. üb. d. Meere, Plateau of Iran 650 toises above the level of the sea.
Tafelland v. Mexico od. Anahuac, Plateau of Mexico or Anahuac.
Taifalen, Taifalæ (tribe on the Danube).
Tajo, Tagus River.
Tambow, Tambov.
Tamesis, Thames River.
Tanais (Danaber), Don River.
Tape, Bostam.
Tapes Ind., Tappe Indians.
Taprobana, Ceylon.
Tarnowitzer Höhe, Plateau of Tarnowitz.
Tarsus, Tersoos.
Tarum, Tarem.
Tatra Gebirg, Tatra Mountains (part of the Carpathian Ms.).
Taurica, Crimea.
Taurien, Tauria.
Taurischer Cherson, Crimea.
Taxila, Attock.
Tay Mündung, Firth of Tay.
Teate, Chieti.
Telmissus, Macry.
Tenerifa, Teneriffe.
Termessus, Schenet.
Teufels Inseln, Devil's Islands.
Thapsacus, Der.
Thebais, Upper Egypt.
Theben, Thebes.
Thebunte, Melhafa.
Themse, Thames River.
Therwinger, Thervingi (Gothic tribe).
Thessalonica, Salonica.
Thracia, Rumilia.
Thrakien (Thracia), Rumilia.
Thuner See, Lake of Thun.
Tiberis, Tevere River.
Tief Sudan, Low Soudan.
Tiefland von Afrika, Lowlands of Africa.
Tingis, Tangiers.
Tischit, Tisheet.
Titianus, Tezzano.
Titicaca See, Lake Titicaca.
Todtes Meer, Dead Sea.
Toletum, Toledo.
Tomi, Tomisvar.
Torneo See u. Elf, Tornea Lake and River.
Torres Strasse, Torres' Strait.
Toscana, Tuscany.
Toskanisches Hochland, Tuscan Highlands.
Transylvanische Alpen, Transylvanian Alps.
Trapezunt, Trebisonde.
Trapezus, Trebisonde.
Tremitische In., Tremiti Islands.
Tridentum, Trento.
Trier, Treves.
Triest, Trieste.
Trileucum, Ortegal.
Troglodyten, Troglodytes (tribe on the Red Sea).
Tschad See, Lake Tchad.
Tscheremissen, Tchermisses (Finnish tribe in Russian Asia).
Tscherkessien, Circassia.
Tschernomorische Kosaken, Cirnomorian Cossacks.
Tschuktschen, Tchookches (tribe in N. E. Asia).
Türkei, Turkey.

Türkisch Croatien, Turkish Croatia.
Tunes, Tunis.
Tungusen, Tungouski (nation in Asia).
Turini, Turin.
Turkmanen, Turcoman (Tartar tribe).
Tusculum, Frascati.
Tyana, Kiliss Hissar.
Tyras, Dniestr River.
Tyras Donaster, Dniestr River.
Tyroler Alpen, Tyrol Alps.
Tyrrhenen, Tyrrheni (Pelasgian tribe).
Tyrrhenisches Meer, Tyrrhenian Sea (part of the Mediterranean).
Tyrus, Soor.

Umgebung von Neu York, Vicinity of New York.
Unerforschte Alpengebirge, Unexplored Mountain Region.
Ungarisches Erzgebirge, Hungarian Erzgebirge.
Ungarn, Hungary.
Unterirdische Wasserleitung, Subterranean Aqueduct.
Unzugängliche Felsenküste, Inaccessible rocky coast.
Ural Gebirge, Oural Mountains.
Uralische Kosaken, Oural Cossacks.
Urumija See, Lake Uromija.
Usa, Ouse River.
Ursprung der Peruanischen Küsten Ström. kalten Wassers, Origin of the Peruvian cold water current.
Uzen, Cumanen oder Polowzer, Utses Camanes or Polovzi (Mongolian tribe).

Vandalen, Vandals (Gothic tribe).
Vanille u. Cacao, Vanilla and Cacao.
Vaterland des Kaffeebaumes, Country of the Coffee tree.
Veldidena, Wilden.
Venedicus Sinus, Gulf of Venice.
Venedig, Venice.
Venetæ, Venetes (tribe in Britany).
Veneten, Venetes (tribe in Britany).
Venetia, Venice.
Vereinigte Staaten, United States.
Verschiedene Ind. Stämme, Various Indian tribes.
Vesuv, Vesuvius.
Vgb. Comaria, Cape Comorin.
Vgb. Maceta, Cape Musseldom.
Vgb. Prionotus, Point Comol.
Vgb. Syagros, Cape Ras Vire.
Viadrus, Oder River.
Viennensis, Dauphiny.

Vierwaldstädter See, Lake of Lucerne.
Vindhy Kette, Vindhya Mountains.
Vindobona, Vienna.
Virunum, Waren.
Visurgis, Weser River.
Vogesen, Vosges Mountains.
Volhynien, Volhynia.
Volubilis, Pharaoh's Castle.
Vorder Rhein, Fore Rhine (one of the rivulets tributary to the Rhine).
Vorgeb Aromata, Cape Guardafui.
Vorgeb Simylla, Cape Simylla.
Votiaken, Wotyaks (Finnish tribe).

Wälder S., Lake of the Woods.
Wahabiten, Wahabites (Mahomedan sect).
Walachei, Walachia.
Waldai Geb., Waldai Mountains.
Walfisch B., Whale Bay.
Wallachisches Tiefland, Wallachian Lowlands.
Wallenstädter See, Lake of Wallenstadt.
Wan See, Lake Van.
Wanger Oge, Wanger Oog.
Warasdiner Geb., Warasdin Mountains.
Warschau, Warsaw.
Weichsel, Vistula River.
Weichsel Niederung, Vistula Lowlands.
Weisse Bai, White Bay.
Weisse Berge, White Mountains.
Weisse Bulgaren, White Bulgarians.
Weisses Meer, White Sea.
Weisses Vorgeb., Cape Blanc.
Weitzen, Gerste u. Hafer, Wheat, Barley and Oats.
Weitzen, Mais und Baumwolle, Wheat, Indian Corn and Cotton.
Weitzen u. Baumwolle, Wheat and Cotton.
Weitzen u. Reis, Wheat and Rice.
Wendekreis des Krebses, Tropic of Cancer.
Wendekreis des Steinbocks, Tropic of Capricorn.
Wenden, Wends (Slavonic tribe).
Wenern See, Lake Wenern.
Wesegothen, Visigoths (nation).
Weser Gb., Weser Mountains.
West Gats, West Ghauts.
West Indien, West Indies.
West Preussen, West Prussia.
West Pyrenäen, West Pyrenees.
West Russland, West Russia.
Wester W., Wester Wald.
Westliche Länge von Paris, W. Longitude from Paris.
Westphalen, Westphalia.

Wettern See, Lake Wettern.
Wien, Vienna.
Wilde Völker, Savage nations.
Windtafel der Griechen nach Aristoteles, Windchart of the Greeks according to Aristotle.
Windtafel der Römer nach Vitruvius, Windchart of the Romans according to Vitruvius.
Winipeg S., Winnipeg Lake.
Winipigoos S., Lake Winnipigoos.
Wogulen, Woguls or Uranfi (Finnish tribe).
Wolga, Volga River.
Wüste al Ahkaf, Desert Al Ahkaf.
Wüste Hochebene, Sandy Plateau.
Wüste Kharasm, Desert of Kharasm.
Wüste Sahara, Desert of Sahara.
Wüste Sahel, Desert of Sahel.
Wüstes Arabien, Arabia Deserta.

Zacynthus, Zante.
Zadracasta, Goorgaun.
Zagrus Geb., Aiagha Mountains.
Zahn u. Elfenbein K., Ivory Coast.
Zalissa, Tiflis.
Zana See, Lake Zana.
Zembre S., Lake Zembe.
Zariaspa später Baetra (Zariaspa, later Baetra), Balkh.
Zeiton, Zeitoun.
Zenobia, Zelebi.
Zephyros (West), West wind.
Zerstückelung des Reiches, Dismembering of the Empire.
Zimmt, Muskatnuss u. Gewürznelke, Cinnamon, Nutmeg, and Clove.
Zucker, Sugar.
Zucker, Kaffee, Thee, Sugar, Coffee, Tea.
Zucker u. Kaffee, Sugar and Coffee.
Züricher See, Lake of Zurich.
Zug unter Gottfried von Bouillon, Crusade under Godfrey of Bouillon.
Zug unter Conrad III. u. Ludwig VII., Crusade under Conrad III. and Louis VII.
Zug unter Ludwig IX. v. Frankr., Crusade under Louis IX. of France.
Zug unter Friedrich Barbarossa, Crusade under Frederick Barbarossa.
Zug unter Kaiser Friedrich II., Crusade under Emperor Frederick II.
Zug unter Richard I. u. Phil. August, Crusade under Richard I. and Philip Augustus.
Zuyder See, Zuyder Zee.
Zwarte Bge., Black Mountains.
Zweibrücken, Bipont.
Zwischen 0° und 10°, Between 0° and 10°.

HISTORY

ANCIENT TIMES AND MIDDLE AGES

PLATE 1.

Egypt.

Fig. 1. The court of the dead
" 2–4. Different trades
" 5. Agriculture
" 6, 7. Hunting and fishing
" 8. Vintage
" 9. King in his chariot
" 10. King on his throne, receiving presents

PLATE 2.

Figs. 1–3. Egyptian costumes
" 4. Lybian costume
" 5. Chinese
" 6–14. Assyrians
" 15, 16. Medes
" 16–20. Persians

PLATE 3.

Figs. 1–4. Egyptian features and head-dresses, from monuments
" 5ab. Heads of male mummies
" 6ab. Heads of female mummies
" 7. Mummy with the inner fillets
" 8. Mummy with the exterior cover
" 9–11. Mummies with the coffins
" 12. Coffin with its cover
" 13, 14. Embalmed animals
" 15, 16. Vases
" 17–19. Large stone vases
" 20ab. Pitchers
" 21, 22. Altars
" 23, 24. Chairs

Fig. 25. Folding chair
" 26, 27. Thrones
" 28, 29. Lounge and footstool
" 30. Knife
" 31. Royal sceptre
" 32, 33. Sphinxes
" 34, 35. Obelisks
" 36. Entrance to the Egyptian labyrinth
" 37–39. Indian pyramids, ground plan elevation, and section
" 40. Rock-tombs near Persepolis

PLATE 4.

Fig. 1. Carthaginian king
" 2. Mauritanian
" 3. Persian woman
" 4–6. Armenians
" 7. Arab
" 8. Phrygian
" 9, 10. Dacians
" 11, 12. Dacian women
" 13. Syrian
" 14. Parthian
" 15. Celtiberian
" 16. Iberian woman
" 17. British woman
" 18–23. Germans

PLATE 5.

Fig. 1. German dwelling
" 2. German infant plunged in the river
" 3. German wedding
" 4–8. Gauls

PLATE 6.

Fig. 1, 2. Egyptian sphinxes
" 3–6. Altars
" 7. Table
" 8–14ab. Pitchers and vases
" 15–19. Cups and other drinking vessels
" 20. Bowl
" 21. Dipper (*Simpulum*)
" 22ab. Royal necklace, and sceptre
" 23, 24. Ethiopian royal headgear
" 25. Numidian " "
" 26. Armenian royal headgear (*Kidaris*)
" 27. Dacian headgear
" 28. Sarmatian headgear
" 29. Scythian royal tiara
" 30, 31. Persian royal tiara
" 32. Assyrian tiara
" 33–37. Indian caps
" 38. Assyrian helmet
" 39. Phrygian cap
" 40ab. Assyrian headgear
" 41, 45b. Indian necklace and girdle
" 42. Chinese imperial cap
" 43–45. Fans and fly-brushes
" 46. Persian covering for the feet
" 47. Persian fan
" 48–50. Persian drinking vessels
" 51. The rock-tomb of Midas in Asia Minor
" 52. Rock-tombs at Persepolis
" 53. Monument near Tortosa in Syria
" 54. Absalom's tomb in the valley of Josaphat, near Jerusalem
" 55–57ab. Carthaginian coins and medals

PLATE 7.

Grecian Costumes.

Figs. 1, 2ab. Maidens
" 3. Youth
" 4. Spinner
" 5. Singer
" 6. Amazon
" 7-13. Women
" 14. Phrygian
" 15, 16. Greeks from Mount Ida
" 17. Philosopher
" 18. Poet
" 19. Prefect
" 20. War-leader

PLATE 8.

Fig. 1. Ceremony at a Greek wedding
" 2. Greek dancer
" 3. Roman funeral ceremony
" 4. Interior of a Greek dwelling
" 5. The Areopagus

PLATE 9.

Figs. 1-6. Games of Greek youth
" 7-24. Olympian games

PLATE 10.

Fig. 1. The philosophers' garden at Athens
" 2-34. Various Grecian articles of furniture
" 35-39. Various Grecian tools
" 40-54. Various Grecian articles of toilet

PLATE 11.

Fig. 1. The rock-tombs of Tarquinii
" 2. Those of Assus
" 3, 4. Those of Ceræa, and their ground plan
" 5, 6. Tombs of Orcla ; elevation
" 7, 8. The same ; the ground plan
" 9, 10. Tombs in Telmessus ; elevation and ground plan
" 11, 12. Tomb in Falerii ; ground plan and section
" 13, 14. Tomb in Agrigentum ; elevation and section
" 15. Tomb from an antique vase
" 16-20. Urns and vases
" 21-23. Tripods
" 24-36ab. Greek coins

PLATE 12.

Rome.

Figs. 1-3. Emperors
" 4, 5. Empresses
" 6, 7. Senators
" 8. Philosopher
" 9. Lictor
" 10. Citizen and his wife
" 11, 12. Youths
" 13-16. Women
" 17-29. Female headgear
" 30-32. Male headgear

PLATE 13.

Rome.

Fig. 1. Exhibition of captives in the forum
" 2. Gladiators in the theatre
" 3. Gladiators at funerals
" 4. Funeral of emperors

PLATE 14.

Figs. 1-16. Details from the Circensian games

PLATE 15.

Fig. 1. Combat with wild beasts in the Coliseum at Rome, under Domitian
" 2-19. Roman consular coins
" 20-25. Roman imperial coins

PLATE 16.

Figs. 1-66. Roman furniture and tools

PLATE 17.

Fig. 1. The street of tombs in Pompeii
" 2-4. Monuments
" 5-7. Sarcophagi
" 8-59. Roman furniture and tools

PLATE 18.

Fig. 1. Gallic women of the Roman time

Figs. 2-6. Bas-reliefs from Gaul
" 7, 8ab. Gallic coins
" 9, 10. Gallic sepulchral urns
" 11-39. Various Gallic trinkets and utensils
" 40-42. German sepulchral urns
" 43-56. Coins, medals, and matrices
" 57, 58. Carthaginian monuments
" 59, 60. Gallic monuments
" 61. The Roman column at Cussy

PLATE 19.

Fig. 1. The Apostles' grotto near Jerusalem
" 2. The catacombs of Syracuse
" 3-6. The catacombs of Naples ; ground plan ; vertical section of a part ; horizontal section of another part ; the chapel
" 7-10. The catacombs of San Marcellino near Rome ; ground plan, perspective view, and details
" 11. Plan of Platonia, near St. Sebastian, before the walls of Rome,
" 12, 13. Tombs of Christian martyrs,
" 14. Christian sarcophagus from the catacombs
" 15. Chapel of St. Hermes
" 16. Chapel of St. Agnes
" 17. Plan of the subterranean church of St. Hermes
" 18. External elevation of the subterranean church of St. Prisca, .
" 19. Tabernacle of the church of St. Nereus and St. Achilleus, near the baths of Antoninus at Rome

PLATE 20.

The Tribes of the Migration.

Fig. 1. Goth
" 2. Sueve
" 3. Gepide
" 4. Vandal
" 5. Marcoman
" 6. Quade
" 7. Herulian
" 8. Briton
" 9. Frank
" 10. Hun
" 11-14. Picts
" 15. Anglo-Saxon chieftain
" 16-18. Anglo-Saxons
" 19. Danish king
" 20. Danish warrior
" 21-23. Danes

PLATE 21.

Costumes of Central Europe.

Fig. 1. Queen Clotilda (6th century)
" 2. Maid of honor
" 3. Frankish leader
" 4ab. Frankish warriors
" 5. King Clovis
" 6. Charlemagne
" 7, 8. Prince and Princess of his house
" 9, 10. Noble and his wife
" 11. Leader under Charlemagne
" 12ab. Warriors
" 13. Bishop
" 14. Common people
" 15-18. Frankish king, queen, prince, and princess
" 19, 20. Prebendary and nun
" 21. Citizen
" 22, 23. Norman king and queen
" 24-26. Norman nobles
" 27, 28. Norman citizen and peasant

PLATE 22.

Figs. 1. 2. Clovis, king of the Franks, and his queen Clotilda
" 3. Fredegonda, from her tomb
" 4. Childebert, king of the Franks
" 5, 6. Statues of Females from the 8th century
" 7. Charlemagne
" 8. Charlemagne receiving the submission of Wittekind
" 9-37. Arms, utensils, and furniture of Charlemagne's time
" 38. Statue of Wittekind
" 39-63. Utensils and furniture of Charlemagne's time

PLATE 23.

Fig. 1. Travelling of Frankish kings in the 8th century
" 2. Manner of transporting wounded or sick princes in the 13th century
" 3. St. Louis administering justice in the open field
" 4. Clerical punishment of French princes in the 13th century
" 5. Vassals paying homage to their liege lord

PLATE 24.

Fig. 1. Full armor of Emperor Maximilian
" 2. Full armor of King Henry VIII.
" 3. English knight
" 4. German knights
" 5. Squires
" 6. English knights in tournament
" 7. German knights before a tournament
" 8. Judge of the tournament

PLATE 25.

Fig. 1. Joust with lances in Germany
" 2. Judicial combat
" 3. Combat with maces in France
" 4. Judicial combat with shields
" 5. Combat with swords
" 6. Combat with lance points
" 7. Carrying the ring in the carrousel
" 8. Squire taking the oath of knighthood on the sword

PLATE 26.

Fig. 1. Young knight taking the solemn oath on the altar
" 2. The ceremony of dubbing a knight

PLATE 27.

Figs. 1-13. Forms of shields
" 14-32. Colors and figures of shields
" 33-43. Divisions of shields
" 64-86. Different crowns
" 87-92. Crests of shields

PLATE 28.

Figs. 1-21. Coats of arms

PLATE 29.

Figs. 1-31. Coats of arms

PLATE 30.

The Inquisition.

Fig. 1. Session of the tribunal
" 2. The punishment of the scourge
" 3. Nailing the hand to the post
" 4. The punishment of strangling
" 5. The fire-torture on the wheel
" 6. Auto-da-fé at Seville

PLATE 31.

The Inquisition

Fig. 1. The torture of the rope and pulley
" 2. The water-torture
" 3. The fire-torture
" 4. Auto-da-fé in Spain

PLATE 32.

Fig. 1. St. Augustin
" 2. St. Antony
" 3, 4. Maronite patriarch and monk
" 5, 6. Armenian patriarch and monk
" 7. St. Basil
" 8. Greek monk in Poland
" 9. Jacobite monk
" 10, 11. Benedictine monk and nun
" 12. Nun of Fontevrault
" 13, 14. Augustine monk and nun
" 15. Prebendary of the Congregation of the Lateran
" 16. Barefoot Carmelite monk
" 17. Carmelite nun
" 18. Carthusian nun
" 19. Calmalduensian monk
" 20. Valombrose monk
" 21. Bernardine nun
" 22, 23. Capuchin monks
" 24. Nun of St. Clarissa
" 25. Sylvestrine monk
" 26, 27. Dominican monk and nun

PLATE 33.

Fig. 1. Monk of the Holy Sepulchre
" 2. Cœlestine monk
" 3. Franciscan monk
" 4. Ursuline nun

Fig. 5. Theatine nun
" 6. Beguine
" 7. Hospitaller of *St. Jacques du haut pas*
" 8. Alexian monk
" 9. Ambrosian monk
" 10. Religious of the order of Jesus
" 11. Annunciate nun
" 12. Nun of "the Immaculate Conception"
" 13. Nun of "the Visitation of St. Mary"
" 14. Nun of "the Word become Flesh"
" 15. Franciscan nun
" 16. Hospital nun of Hotel-Dieu in Paris
" 17. Jesuit
" 18. Jesuit missionary in China
" 19. Sister of Charity
" 20. Bethlehemite monk
" 21. Priest of the Oratory in France
" 22. Doctrinary
" 23. Barnabite monk
" 24. Priest of the pious schools of France and Belgium
" 25, 26. Feuillantine monk and nun
" 27. Monk of St. Maurus

PLATE 34.

Fig. 1. Visitantine nun in Flanders
" 2. Nun of "*Notre-Dame*"
" 3. Nun of "*Notre Dame de la Miséricorde*"

Fig. 4. Priest of the Congregation of Missions
" 5. Sister of Charity of St. Vincent de Paula
" 6. Hospital nun of *La Flèche*
" 7*a*. Trappist monk
" 7*b*. Poor volunteer monk of Flanders
" 8. Grand master of the Order of Malta
" 9. Grand cross of the same
" 10. Knight of Malta
" 11. Lady of the Order of St. John of Jerusalem
" 12. Templar in house dress
" 13. Templar in war costume
" 14. Templar in full armor mounted
" 15. Grand master of the German Knights
" 16. Knight of St. James of the Sword
" 17. Knight of the Order of Calatrava
" 18. Knight of the Order of Alcantara
" 19. Knight of St. Avis in Portugal
" 20. Knight of St. Stephen
" 21. Knight of the Holy Ghost
" 22. Hospitaller of the Holy Ghost
" 23. Religious of the Order d'Aubrac

PLATE 35.
Freemasonry.

Fig. 1. Initiation of apprentice
" 2. Initiation of master
" 3. Initiation of the 33d degree of the Scottish lodge

Fig. 4. Funeral of a companion

PLATE 36.

Fig. 1. Hawking in France
" 2. Departure of crusaders for Palestine

PLATE 37.

Fig. 1. Combat between crusaders and Saracens
" 2. Harangue to crusaders before the walls of Jerusalem

PLATE 38.

Fig. 1. Return of crusaders from Palestine
" 2. Tournament in Germany

PLATE 39.

Fig. 1. Ground plan of the church of St. Mary of the Manger at Bethlehem
" 2. Interior of the church of St. Mary of the Manger in Bethlehem, with the entrance to the chapel of the Holy Grotto
" 3. Interior of the chapel with the Holy Grotto
" 4. Ground plan of the church of the Holy Sepulchre in Jerusalem
" 5. Portico and entrance to the same
" 6. Interior of the same, with the Holy Chapel

ETHNOLOGY

ETHNOLOGY OF THE PRESENT DAY

PLATE 1.
The Five Principal Races.
1. *Caucasian Race.*

Fig. 1. Inhabitants of Central Europe
" 2. Greek
" 3. Turk
" 4. Cossack
" 5. Persian
" 6. Hindoo
" 7. Bedouin
" 8, 9. Cabyles
2. *Mongolian Race.*
Fig. 10. Kalmuck
" 11. Chinese
" 12. Samoyede
" 13. Esquimaux
3. *Ethiopian Race.*
Fig. 14. Guinea Negro
" 15. Boussa Negro
" 16. Hottentot
" 23, 24. Papuas (Australia)
4. *American Race.*
Figs. 17–21. Indians
5. *Malay Race.*
Fig. 22. Native of New Zealand

PLATE 2.

Fig. 1. Peasant girl from Baden
" 2. Peasant from the Baden highlands
" 3, 4. Inhabitants of the Black Forest
" 5–9. Wirtembergers
" 10–15. Bavarians
" 16, 17. Hessians
" 18, 19. Inhabitants of Rhenish Prussia
" 20. Inhabitants of Brunswick
" 21, 22. Inhabitants of the District of Coblentz (Rhine)
" 23, 24. Inhabitants of Altenburg (Saxony)

PLATE 3.

Fig. 1. Inhabitants of the District of Erfurt (Thuringia)
" 2. Inhabitants of Holstein
" 3. Inhabitants of the District of Lüneburg (Hanover)
" 4, 5. Inhabitants of the District of Hamburg
" 6–8. Inhabitants of East Friesland (Hanover)
" 9–11. Inhabitants of Silesia
" 12–15. Inhabitants of Tyrol

Figs. 16–19. Inhabitants of Austria
" 20–22. Inhabitants of Styria
" 23. Inhabitants of Bohemia
" 24. Inhabitants of Illyria

PLATE 4.
Upper Division.
Figs. 1–12. The German gymnasium
Lower Division.
Figs. 1–8. Acrobatic feats

PLATE 5.
Figs. 1–3. Equestrian feats

PLATE 6.
Figs. 1, 2. Horse races
" 3. Masked ball at Paris

PLATE 7.
Fig. 1. Grand promenade in the Elysian Fields (Paris)
" 2. Festival at St. Petersburg
" 3. Public meeting in England

PLATE 8.
Fig. 1. Naumachy on the Seine in Paris
" 2. Rural ball
" 3. Illumination in Rome

PLATE 9.
Fig. 1. Spanish barn
" 2. Sardinian barn
" 3. Sardinian wedding
" 4. The Bolero (Spanish dance)
" 5. Spanish bull-fight

PLATE 10.
Russian Tribes.
Figs. 1, 2. Strielzi
" 3. Russo-Polish guard
" 4–7. Inhabitants of Little Russia
" 8–10. Fishermen from the Volga
" 11. Inhabitants of Novgorod
" 12, 13. Inhabitants of the district of Twer
" 14. Inhabitants of the Ukraine
" 15. Cossack of the Don
" 16. Inhabitants of the district of Moscow
Caucasian Tribes.
Figs. 17–22. Circassians
" 23. Turkoman
" 24. Abasian
" 25. Mingrelian
" 26. Imeritian

Fig. 27. Georgian

PLATE 11.
Figs. 1, 2. Russian rural games
" 3. Russian public bath
" 4, 5. Russian large and small knout

PLATE 12.
Fig. 1. Russian sleighing and gliding hill
" 2. Russian serfs on the Don
" 3. Russian national dance
" 4. Festivity at Pergola (Russia)
" 5. Lapland winter cabins

PLATE 13.
Fig. 1 *a–s.* Oriental headgear
" 2. Syrians
" 3, 4. Smyrnese
" 5–8. Maronites
" 9. Girl of Nablous
" 10. Nazarenes
" 11–15. Arabs
" 16, 17. Armenians
" 18. Turk of Mardin

PLATE 14.
Fig. 1. Public baths for women in Turkey
" 2. Interior of a harem
" 3. Supper at the grand vizier's
" 4. Ceremony in the sultan's presence chamber
" 5. Dance of the dervises
" 6. Prayer and ablution of the Mahomedans
" 7. Penitent dervise

PLATE 15.
Figs. 1–9. Persians
" 10. Beludshis
" 11. Usbek
" 12. Afghan
" 13. Kurd
" 14. Kirghis
" 15. Imeritian
" 16. Georgian
" 17. Mingrelian
" 18. Caucasian mountaineer

PLATE 16.
Figs. 1–3. Bashkirs and Kirghis in camp
" 4–6. Tartars
" 7, 8. Kurds
" 9. Persian nobleman

PLATE 17.
Fig. 1. Wedding in Persia

Fig. 2. Persian women travelling
" 3. Persian music
" 4. Persian meal
" 5. Persian game
" 6, 7. Persian punishments

PLATE 18.

Fig. 1. Rajah of Cutch and his vassals (English East Indies)
" 2. Caravan in Kattiavar (English East Indies)

PLATE 19.

Fig. 1. Arabian nomades
" 2. Bedouin camp
" 3, 4. Arabian music and dance
" 5, 6. Travelling in Lahore

PLATE 20.

Figs. 1–3. Indian women and girls
" 4. Slave of a harem
" 5. Indian harem
" 6. Car festival in India
" 7. Salutation of the Arabians
" 8. Persian funeral

PLATE 21.

Fig. 1. Penitent Hindoo fanatic
" 2. Burning of a Hindoo widow with the remains of her husband
" 3. Wedding ceremony of the Tzingaris (Indian gipsies)
" 4. Nuptial procession of wealthy Hindoos

PLATE 22.

Figs. 1–6. Chinese
" 7. Corean
" 8. Loo-Choo islander
" 9–14. Japanese

PLATE 23.

Fig. 1. Tea culture in China
" 2. Silk culture in China
" 3. Chinese rice-dealer

PLATE 24.

Fig. 1. Chinese jugglers
" 2. Chinese theatre
" 3. Chinese punishment

PLATE 25.

Fig. 1. Chinese puppet-show
" 2. Chinese mandarin visiting
" 3. Chinese quack

PLATE 26.

Fig. 1. Moorish baths in Algiers
" 2, 3. Moorish noble and merchant
" 4. Arabian chief in Algiers
" 5. Jewess of Algiers
" 6. Slave
" 7. Lady of Cairo
" 8. Girl of Bornou (Senegal)
" 9. Negro king of Boussa
" 10, 11. Girls of Timbuktoo and Sokna (Fez)
" 12. Idolatry in Central Africa

PLATE 27.

Fig. 1. Egyptian Fellahs
" 2. Arabian dames and tents
" 3. Bedouins

Fig. 4, 5. Arabian caravan
" 6. Nuptial procession in Cairo

PLATE 28.

Fig. 1. Abyssinian costumes
" 2. Abyssinian travelling
" 3. Elephant hunting
" 4. Negro chief and suite
" 5. Negro funeral south of the Coango River
" 6. Christian negro-women of Benguela
" 7. Negro soldier (Portuguese Africa)
" 8. Molua negroes guarding their king's dwelling
" 9. Human sacrifices of the Cassange negroes

PLATE 29.

Figs. 1–7. Sports of Indian tribes

PLATE 30.

Fig. 1. Mexican
" 2, 3. Inhabitants of La Puebla
" 4. Woman of Jalapa
" 5, 6. Costumes of Guatemala
" 7. Rich mulatto woman
" 8. Brazilian Mestizo
" 9, 10. Costumes of Bolivia
" 11. Girl of Bogota
" 12. Girl of Lima
" 13. Squaw of the district of Quito
" 14. Muleteers of the Cordilleras
" 15, 16. Costumes of La Conception
" 17. Costumes of Chili
" 18. Gaucho of Buenos Ayres

PLATE 31.

Fig. 1. Travelling farmer from the Rio Grande in Brazil
" 2. Traveller from the province of Minas
" 3. Brazilian planter's family driving to mass
" 4. Townsmen from the Brazilian Rio Grande travelling
" 5. Caravan of Brazilian merchants
" 6. Convoy of diamonds

PLATE 32.

Fig. 1. Brazil Camacans in the forest
" 2. Festivity of the Camacans
" 3. Negroes from Bahia
" 4. Free negro bringing up a fugitive slave
" 5. Inhabitants of San Paulo
" 6, 7. Civilized Paraguay Indians

PLATE 33.

Fig. 1. Brazilian plantation
" 2, 3. Diamond washing
" 4, 5. Brazilian sports
" 6. Brazilian planter's family walking to mass
" 7. Patagonian camp

PLATE 34.

Figs. 1–6. Brazilian slave trade

PLATE 35.

Fig. 1. Greenland seal-hunting
" 2. Brazilian Indians bird-shooting

Fig. 3. Attack by Guaycouros horsemen (Brazil)
" 4. Cattle-hunting on the Pampas (Brazil)
" 5. Negro dances at San Paulo
" 6. South Patagonian huts and graves

PLATE 36.

Figs. 1–4. Sports of Brazilian Indians
" 5ab. Duels and combats among the Botocudos
" 6. Duel among the Purvis

PLATE 37.

Fig. 1. Human sacrifice of the ancient Mexicans
" 2. Cannibals of the Paraguay forests
" 3. Cannibals preparing a peculiar beverage
" 4–6. War-dance, execution of captives, and funeral with the Tupinambas

PLATE 38.

Figs. 1, 2. Funeral of a chief (Sandwich Islands)
" 3. Funeral in New Zealand
" 4. Tahitian girl, carrying presents
" 5. Dance of the Tahitians
" 6. Dance of the aborigines of the Caroline Islands

PLATE 39.

Fig. 1. Chief from the Tonga islands
" 2. Combat of Tonga women
" 3–5. Girlish sports on the Tonga islands
" 6. Dance of Australian aborigines
" 7–9. Wedding ceremony, funeral and ball of Australian aborigines
" 10. Ceremony of the Gna-Lung

PLATE 40.

Fig. 1. War dance of the Booro islanders.
" 2. Cock-fight on the Philippine islands
" 3. Making brandy on the Marian islands
" 4. Caroline islander
" 5, 6. Aborigines of New Zealand
" 7. Dance of the same

PLATE 41.

Fig. 1. Ceremonial salutation among the aborigines of New Zealand
" 2. Tattooing of the same
" 3. Indian and his squaw from the Caroline islands
" 4. Dance of the Indians of this tribe
" 5–7. Indians of the island of Hawaï
" 8. Dance of Australian savages

PLATE 42.

Fig. 1. Dance in Samoa
" 2. Dwelling of the Chinooks
" 3. Meeting on Drummond's island

MILITARY SCIENCES

PLATE 1.

Figs. 1–22. Weapons of the Egyptians
" 23–56. Weapons of the Medes and Persians

PLATE 2.

Fig. 1. Grecian hero
" 2. Amazon from the Black Sea
" 3–8. Grecian warriors on foot
" 9. Grecian trumpeter
" 10. Grecian combat
" 11. Grecian herald
" 12, 13. Grecian horsemen
" 14. Etruscan archer
" 15. Etruscan hornblower
" 16–18. Etruscan soldiers

PLATE 3.

Figs. 1–21. Weapons of the Greeks

Figs. 22–35. Weapons of the Etruscans
" 36–50. Weapons of the Romans

PLATE 4.

Figs. 1–30. Illustrating the movements of Grecian troops
" 31–51. Illustrating the movements of Roman troops

PLATE 5.

Fig. 1. Grecian funeral and death feast
" 2. Roman imperator and suite
" 3. The war-elephant in combat
" 4. Armed chariot

PLATE 6.

Fig. 1. Funeral procession of Alexander the Great
" 2. Triumphal procession of a Roman general

PLATE 7.

Figs. 1–5. Roman Italian allies
" 6, 7. German allies
" 8. Roman trumpeter
" 9. Roman hornblower
" 10. Roman slinger
" 11. Roman lancers
" 12. Velites
" 13–19. Various ranks in the Roman army

PLATE 8.

Fig. 1. Roman imperator
" 2. Roman general
" 3. Roman lictor
" 4. The Imperator's body-guard
" 5. Sarmatian mailed horseman
" 6. Roman legate

Fig. 7. Roman standard-bearers
" 8. Roman decurion of cavalry
" 9. Roman cavalry soldier

PLATE 9.
Figs. 1–46. Weapons of the Gauls, Franks, Germans, Britons, Anglo-Saxons, and Anglo-Danes
" 47. Roman saddle
" 48. Anglo-Saxon saddle
" 49–62. Various saddles of the middle ages
" 63, 64. Spurs of the fourteenth century

PLATE 10.
Figs. 1, 2. Roman legion eagles
" 3, 4. Standards
" 5–15. Field badges
" 16–23. Honorary crowns
" 24, 25. Honorary medals
" 26, 27. Trophies
" 28. Trajan's column

PLATE 11.
Fig. 1. Roman prisoners passing under the yoke
" 2. Roman victor thanking the army
" 3–5. Triumphal processions

PLATE 12.
Fig. 1. The war dance of German youths
" 2. Ceremony of bestowing the right to bear arms
" 3. Ceremony of soothsaying before battle
" 4. Germans in combat

PLATE 13.
Fig. 1. Roman camp
" 2. Roman order of battle
" 3. The solid wedge
" 4. The boar's head
" 5. The tortoise
" 6. Carthaginian order of battle with elephants

PLATE 14.
Fig. 1. Decimation of prisoners
" 2. Election of commander
" 3. Combat of infantry against cavalry

PLATE 15.
Figs. 1–77. Weapons of the Germans, Normans, Anglo-Saxons, and Danes

PLATE 16.
Figs. 1–23. Armor of the middle ages

PLATE 17.
Fig. 1. Emperor's suit of armor
" 2. Elector's suit of armor
" 3, 4. Knights' armor
" 5, 6. Footsoldiers
" 7–10. Tourney equipments
" 11. Awarding the prize at a tourney

PLATE 18.
Figs. 1–10. Different dignitaries of the war-ban
" 11. The marching forth of an army from its camp

PLATE 19.
Upper Division.
Figs. 1–14. Prussian infantry
Lower Division.
Figs. 1–12. French infantry

PLATE 20.
Upper Division.
Figs. 1–10. Prussian cavalry
Lower Division.
Figs. 11–19. French cavalry

PLATE 21.
Upper Division.
Figs. 1–8. Austrian infantry
Lower Division.
Figs. 1–11. British infantry

PLATE 22.
Figs. 1–9. British cavalry
" 10–20. Belgian cavalry, artillery, and engineers

PLATE 23.
Figs. 1–10. Troops of the older Turkish military system
" 11–17. Modern Turkish army

PLATE 24.
Fig. 1. Turkish pasha and suite
" 2. Encampment of a pasha of three tails
" 3. Body-guard
" 4, 5. Turkish warlike games

PLATE 25.
Figs. 1–60. Illustrating the various kinds of arms of modern times

PLATE 26.
Figs. 1–41. Illustrating military gymnastics

PLATE 27.
Figs. 1–48. Illustrating military fencing

PLATE 28.
Figs. 1–18. Practical exercises in fencing

PLATE 29.
Figs. 1–47. Illustrating modern tactics
" 48. Disembarkation of French troops in Algiers

PLATE 30.
Upper Division.
Figs. 1–13. Austrian orders
Lower Division.
Figs. 1–11. Prussian orders

PLATE 31.
Figs. 1–4. Bavarian orders
" 5, 6. Saxon orders
" 7–9. Hanoverian orders
" 10–12. Wirtemberg orders
" 13–15. Orders of Baden
" 16, 17. Orders of Electoral Hesse
" 18, 19. Orders of the grand-duchy of Hesse
" 20, 21. The Danish Dannebrog order
" 22. Order of the white falcon
" 23. Order of the Saxe-Ernestine house
" 24, 25. Orders of Saxe-Altenburg
" 26. War medal of Saxe-Meiningen
" 27. War medal of Saxe-Hildburghausen
" 28. War medal of Saxe-Gotha-Altenburg
" 29–31. Orders of Brunswick and Nassau
" 32. Mecklenburg order
" 33. Oldenburg order
" 34. War medal of Anhalt Köthen
" 35. Volunteer's cross of Anhalt Dessau

PLATE 32.
Figs. 1, 2. French orders
" 3, 4. British orders
" 5, 6. Russian orders
" 7, 8. Turkish orders
" 9. Persian order
" 10, 11. Spanish order
" 12. Portuguese order
" 13. Neapolitan order
" 14, 15. Sardinian orders
" 16. Papal order
" 17. Tuscan order
" 18. Grecian order
" 19. Belgian order
" 20, 21. Swedish orders
" 22, 23. Dutch orders
" 24. The Danish elephant-order
" 25. Brazilian order

PLATE 33.
Figs. 1–18. Ancient military engines

PLATE 34.
Figs. 1–24. Military engines of the middle ages

PLATE 35.
Fig. 1. Watch tower

Fig. 2. Siege tower
" 3–6. Movable towers
" 7. Ancient trenches
" 8. The storming ram
" 9. The lifting forceps
" 10. Drawbasket
" 11. Storming a wall

PLATE 36.
Figs. 1–41. Illustrating modern artillery

PLATE 37.
Figs. 1–34. Illustrating artillery carriages

PLATE 38.
Figs. 1–24. Illustrating artillery and pontoon carriages

PLATE 39.
Figs. 1–50. Illustrating the fabrication of artillery and projectiles, balls and bombs

PLATE 40.
Figs. 1–57. Illustrating military pyrotechny

PLATE 41.
Fig. 1. Roman fortified camp
" 2. Scipio's circumvallation of Numantia
" 3. Cæsar's siege of Massilia

PLATE 42.
Figs. 1–4. The simplest ancient gates, 616
" 5. The Gate of the Lions in Mycenæ,
" 6–9. The walls of Messene
" 10, 11. The gate of Spello
" 12, 13. The walls of Babylon
" 14, 15. The walls of Assos
" 16. The gates of Falerii
" 17. The Appian gate of Rome
" 18. Gate at Pompeii
" 19, 20. Sections of the walls of Rome,

PLATE 43.
Figs. 1–5. Walls between Athens and the Piræus
" 6. The Capitoline hill
" 7–9. Details of the walls
" 10–15. The walls of Pompeii

PLATE 44.
Fig. 1. Ditch of a castle
" 2. Dungeon
" 3. Oubliette
" 4. Turret
" 5, 6. Plan and view of tower stairs
" 7. Lantern
" 8. Tower window
" 9. Magazine under a dungeon
" 10. Machicolis
" 11–13. Drawbridges
" 14, 15. Castle of Vincennes, plan and view
" 16. Castle of Rheinstein

PLATE 45.
Fig. 1. The Chinese wall
" 2–4. Different towers
" 5–10. Battlements
" 12–14. Loopholes

PLATE 46.
Fig. 1. Fortified bridge
" 2–7. Fortified gates
" 8–10. The Bastille in Paris
" 11. The old Louvre in Paris
" 12–21. Various forms of loopholes

PLATE 47.
Figs. 1–57. Illustrating field fortification

PLATE 48.
Figs. 1–42. Illustrating permanent fortifications

PLATE 49.
Figs. 1–37. Illustrating attack and defence of fortified places

PLATE 50.
Figs. 1–51. Illustrating attack and defence of fortified places

PLATE 51.
Figs. 1–54. Illustrating the pioneer and pontoon service

PLATE 1.

Figs. 1, 2. Phœnician vessels
" 3, 4. Prows
" 5. Stern-figure (aplustre)
" 6, 7. Prow-figures
" 8. Hiero's show-ship
" 9. Vessel used in the Roman Naumachia
" 10. Ship with a tower
" 11–14. Roman vessels of war
" 15. Norman vessel of war
" 16. Roman sea-fight

PLATE 2.

Fig. 1. Egyptian boat
" 2. Phœnician vessel
" 3, 4. Greek vessels
" 5, 6. Greek vessels
" 7. Roman vessel
" 8. Greek prow
" 9. Egyptian vessel
" 10. Cleopatra's show-ship
" 11. Ptolemy's show-ship
" 12. Roman Naumachia
" 13, 14. Anchors
" 15. Rudder
" 16. Oar
" 17. Oar-holes
" 18. Prow
" 19. Lighthouse
" 19 a–d. Ground-plans of the lighthouse
" 20–24. Coins showing lighthouses
" 25. Naval Column

PLATE 3.

Fig. 1. French vessel of the 16th century
" 2. Genoese prow
" 3. Spanish ship of war
" 4. The Sovereign of the Seas
" 5. Soleil royal
" 6. Venetian galley
" 7. The ship Ocean

PLATE 4.

Fig. 1. Portuguese carac
" 2. The Great Harry
" 3. Stern of a ship
" 4. French galley
" 5. Observatory
" 6. Lighthouse
" 7, 8. French cutters
" 9. English cutter
" 10. Bomb ketch
" 11. Felucca

PLATE 5.

Fig. 1. European factory at Canton
" 2. Chinese war penish
" 3. The same under sail
" 4, 5. Chinese coasters
" 6, 7. Chinese gondolas
" 8. Chinese junk
" 9. Coaster of the Maldives
" 10. Malay coaster
" 11. Malay anchor
" 12, 13. Malacca vessels
" 14. Java vessel

PLATE 6.

Fig. 1. Macao vessel
" 2. Chinese coaster
" 3. Malacca vessel
" 4, 5. Vessels of the Moluccas
" 6. Java coaster
" 7, 8. Vessels of the Coromandel
coast
" 9, 10. Manilla coasters
" 11, 12. Coasters of the Philippine
islands
" 13, 14. Coasters of Celebes

PLATE 7.

Figs. 1–33. Illustrating the theory of ship-
building

PLATE 8.

Fig. 1. Ship of the line on the stocks
" 2. Launch of a ship of the line
" 3. Caulking of a vessel
" 4. Graving of a vessel
" 5. Rope-walk
" 6. Sail bench

PLATE 9.

Fig. 1. Longitudinal section of a ship of
the line
" 2. Transverse section of the same
" 3. Iron knee
" 4. Construction of a ship's stern
" 5. Construction of deck
" 6–25. Illustrating Seppings's system
of ship-building
" 26. A capstan
" 27. Longitudinal section of a ship of
the line, showing its interior
arrangement, 691, 699, 701, 702, 723

PLATE 10.

Fig. 1. View from above of the lower gun
deck
" 2. View from above of the upper deck
" 3. French frigate
" 4. Topsail-yard and topgallant
sail
" 5, 6. Fore-and-aft sails
" 7. A vane
" 8, 9. Pennants
" 10. A ship's pump
" 11. A windlass
" 12, 13. Details of the same
" 14–29. Anchors
" 30. Splicing cables
" 31, 32. Anchor-buoys
" 33. Mushroom anchor

PLATE 11.

Fig. 1. French ship of the line,
showing the outfit of a
ship
" 2. Normandy fishing-smack
" 3. Mainyard with its jeers
" 4. Upper part of a mainmast
" 5, 6. Caps
" 7. Dead-eyes
" 8. Tackle with runner
" 9. Winding tackle in threefold
blocks
" 10–16. Various blocks and dead-eyes
" 17, 18. Pitch ladles
" 19 Axe
" 20. Pole-axe
" 21. Scraper
" 22. Double scraper
" 23. Horse-bit
" 24. Adze
" 25. Hatchet
" 26, 27. Caulking tools
" 28, 29. Trucks
" 30. Knobbed rope
" 31, 32ab. Caulking mallets
" 33. Tar brush
" 34. Callipers
" 35–40. Implements for serving guns
" 41–49. Various kinds of shot

PLATE 12.

Fig. 1. Main forward deck of a French
ship of the line
" 2. The after-deck
" 3. Lengthwise view of a French two-
decker, with a portion of the
planking removed

PLATE 13.
FLAGS OF VARIOUS NATIONS.

The colors of the flags are indicated by the
different lines and dots marked at the foot of
the plate: Gelb meaning yellow; Roth, red;
Hellblau, light blue; Dunkelblau, dark blue;
Schwarz, black; Hellgrün, light green; Dunkelgrün, dark green; Purpur, purple; Braun,
brown.

Fig. 1. Kingdom of Great Britain.
" 2. Kingdom of France under L. Philippe.
" 3. Empire of Russia.
" 4. Empire of Austria.
" 5. Kingdom of Spain.
" 6. Kingdom of Portugal.
" 7. Kingdom of Holland.
" 8. Kingdom of Sweden and Norway.
" 9. Kingdom of Prussia.
" 10. Kingdom of Denmark.
" 11. Kingdom of Naples.
" 12. Kingdom of Hanover.
" 13. British red flag.
" 14. British white flag.

Fig. 15. British blue flag.
" 16. British admiralty's flag.
" 17. British admiral's flag.
" 18. East India Company's flag.
" 19. Republic of the Ionian islands.
" 20. Maltese flag.
" 21. French commercial flag.
" 22. Franco-Algerine flag.
" 23. Russian naval flag.
" 24. Russo-American flag.
" 25. Russian commercial flag.
" 26. Austrian naval and commercial flag.
" 27. Austro-Venetian flag.
" 28. Spanish naval flag.
" 29. Spanish commercial flag.
" 30. Spanish-Philippine commercial flag.
" 31. Portuguese naval and commercial flag.
" 32. Dutch commercial flag.
" 33. Dutch Batavian flag.
" 34. Norwegian national flag.
" 35. Swedish naval flag.
" 36. Swedish commercial flag.
" 37. Prussian naval flag.
" 38. Prussian commercial flag.
" 39. Danish naval flag.
" 40. Danish commercial flag.
" 41. Schleswig-Holstein flag.
" 42. Hamburg admiralty flag.
" 43. Hamburg commercial flag.
" 44. Old Lubec naval flag.
" 45. Lubec commercial flag.
" 46. Bremen commercial flag.
" 47. Hanoverian commercial flag.
" 48. Oldenburg commercial flag.
" 49. Mecklenburg commercial flag.
" 50. Belgian naval and commercial flag.
" 51. Flag of the Saxon river cities.
" 52. Flag of the Bavarian river cities.
" 53. Flag of the Wirtemberg river cities.
" 54. Flag of the Baden river cities.
" 55. Swiss flag.
" 56. Flag of Frankfort on the Main.
" 57. Hungarian flag.
" 58. Servian flag.
" 59. Moldavian flag.
" 60. Wallachian flag.
" 61. Neapolitan naval and commercial flag.
" 62. Papal flag.
" 63. Tuscan naval and commercial flag.
" 64. Leghorn flag.
" 65. Flag of Lucca.
" 66. Flag of Massa-Carrara.
" 67. Flag of Modena.
" 68. Flag of Monaco.
" 69. Royal Sardinian flag.
" 70. Sardinian naval and commercial flag.
" 71. Old Genoese flag.
" 72. Old Savoy flag.
" 73. Flag of the island of Sardinia.
" 74. Greek naval flag.
" 75. Greek commercial flag.
" 76. Greek pirate's flag.
" 77. Turkish imperial flag.
" 78. Turkish naval flag.
" 79. Turkish commercial flag.
" 80. Flag of the grand vizier.
" 81. Flag of Capudan Pasha.
" 82. Comm. flag of Tunis, Tripoli, Morocco.
" 83. Flag of Tunis.
" 84. Flag of Morocco.
" 85. Flag of the viceroy of Egypt.
" 86. Egyptian commercial flag.
" 87. Flag of Tripoli.
" 88. Old Algerine flag.
" 89. Algerine pirate's flag.
" 90. Arabian flag.
" 91. Abyssinian flag.
" 92. The flag of the Shah of Persia.
" 93. Persian commercial flag.
" 94. Flag of Afghanistan.
" 95. Flag of Beloochistan.
" 96. Flag of the Great Mogul.
" 97. Flag of Bengal.
" 98. Flag of Scind.
" 99. Flag of the Birmans.
" 100. Flag of Pegu.
" 101. Flag of Siam.
" 102. Flag of Sumatra.
" 103. Chinese imperial flag.
" 104, 105. Chinese commercial flags.
" 106. Flag of Cochin-China.
" 107. Japanese imperial flag.
" 108. Commercial flag of Japan.

Fig. 109. Flag of the United States, N. A.
" 110. Flag of Texas.
" 111. Flag of Mexico.
" 112. Flag of Guatemala.
" 113. Flag of Hayti.
" 114. Flag of Columbia.
" 115. Flag of Venezuela.
" 116. Flag of Bolivia.
" 117. Flag of Peru.
" 118. Flag of Chili.
" 119. Flag of Brazil.
" 120. Flag of La Plata.
" 121. Flag of Equador.
" 122. Flag of Otaheite.
" 123. Flag of the Sandwich Islands.
" 124. Flag of New Zealand.

PLATE 14.
Fig. 1. A galliot
" 2. An English lugger
" 3. A sloop of war
" 4. French frigate
" 5. French ship of the line
" 6. Prison ship

PLATE 15.
Fig. 1. Newfoundland fisherman
" 2. Havre de Grace fishing-smack
" 3. Coaster of the Mediterranean
" 4. French coaster
" 5. Mediterranean xebec
" 6. Mediterranean pink
" 7. Danish coaster
" 8. A galliot
" 9. Dutch brig galliot
" 10. A barque
" 11. Slave ship
" 12. After part of a French merchant-
man

PLATE 16.
Fig. 1. A cutter
" 2. Hermaphrodite brig
" 3. Barque taking in freight
" 4. Whale ship
" 5. Emigrant ship
" 6. The Bremen steamboat Guten-
burg
" 7. The American steamship Wash-
ington

PLATE 17.
Fig. 1. Spanish gun-boat
" 2. French iron steam propeller
" 3. English war cutter
" 4. Swedish brig of war
" 5. English brig of war
" 6. French steam frigate

PLATE 18.
Figs. 1–22 Illustrating the construction of
steamships

PLATE 19.
Figs. 1–31. Illustrating the construction of
steamships

PLATE 20.
Figs. 1–5. French naval officers
" 6–10. Russian naval officers
" 11–13. English naval officers
" 14. Naval cadet (midshipman)
" 15–19. Sailors, boatswains, &c.,

PLATE 21.
Fig. 1. Officer on watch
" 2. The wheel
" 3. Middle deck
" 4. Starboard battery at night
" 5. Starboard battery in daytime
" 6. Midshipmen's cabin

PLATE 22.
Fig. 1. Forward part of a French frigate
" 2. After part of a French frigate
" 3. Carronade with its carriage
" 4. Gun with its carriage
" 5. Port-guard
" 6. Davits with lifting tackle

PLATE 23.
Fig. 1. Caulking shot holes
" 2. Look-out from the topsail yard
" 3. Taking in sail and reefing
" 4. Throwing the lead
" 5. Hoisting out a boat
" 6. Heaving the log
" 7. Cleaning the deck

PLATE 24.
Fig. 1. Court-martial
" 2. Keel-hauling
" 3. Hoisting the flag
" 4. Ship on fire

PLATE 25.
Fig. 1. English ship of the line firing a
salute
" 2. French ship of the line in flag
parade
" 3. Hoisting flag in running into port,
" 4. Striking flag in surrendering
" 5. Night signals
" 6. Top-men
" 7. Sailors playing cards
" 8. Confinement in irons

PLATE 26.
Fig. 1. Ship signalizing with flags
" 2. Ship drying sail

Fig. 3. Ship inclosed with ice
" 4. Ship with all sails set
" 5. Ship setting sail
" 6. Ship getting under weigh
" 7. Ship bracing round
" 8ab. Ships sailing on a half wind
" 9ab. Ships going about
" 10. Ships bearing to windward
" 11. Ships shortening sail
" 12. Ship of the line under short sail

PLATE 27.
Fig. 1. Ships getting under weigh
" 2. Ships pitching
" 3. Barque rolling
" 4. Barque under close-reefed top-
sails
" 5. Barque thrown on one side
" 6. Shipwreck

PLATE 28.
Figs. 1–35. Illustrating manœuvres of
fleets

PLATE 29.
Fig. 1. Manœuvres by schooners
" 2. Steamer of war carrying de-
spatches
" 3. Line of battle
" 4. Naval battle

PLATE 30.
Fig. 1. Drydock in Toulon
" 2. Towing a vessel into port
" 3. Ship-ways dry at ebb tide
" 4. Graving-dock
" 5–7. Diving-bells
" 8, 9. Steam dredgers

PLATE 31.
Fig. 1, 2. Roadsteads
" 3. Crane for setting masts
" 4. Pile-driving machine
" 5. Naval arsenal
" 6. Common dredging machine

PLATE 32.
Fig. 1. Ground plan of the West India
docks in London
" 2. Ground plan of the harbor of
Toulon
" 3–6. Prince's docks at Liverpool
" 7. Profile of the wall of the London
docks
" 8. Profile of the Mersey quay at Liverpool
" 9–12. Dundee dry dock
" 13–17. The lighthouse of Trieste
" 18. Lighthouse of Bell rock (vertical
section)
" 13–23. Iron lighthouse at Bermuda

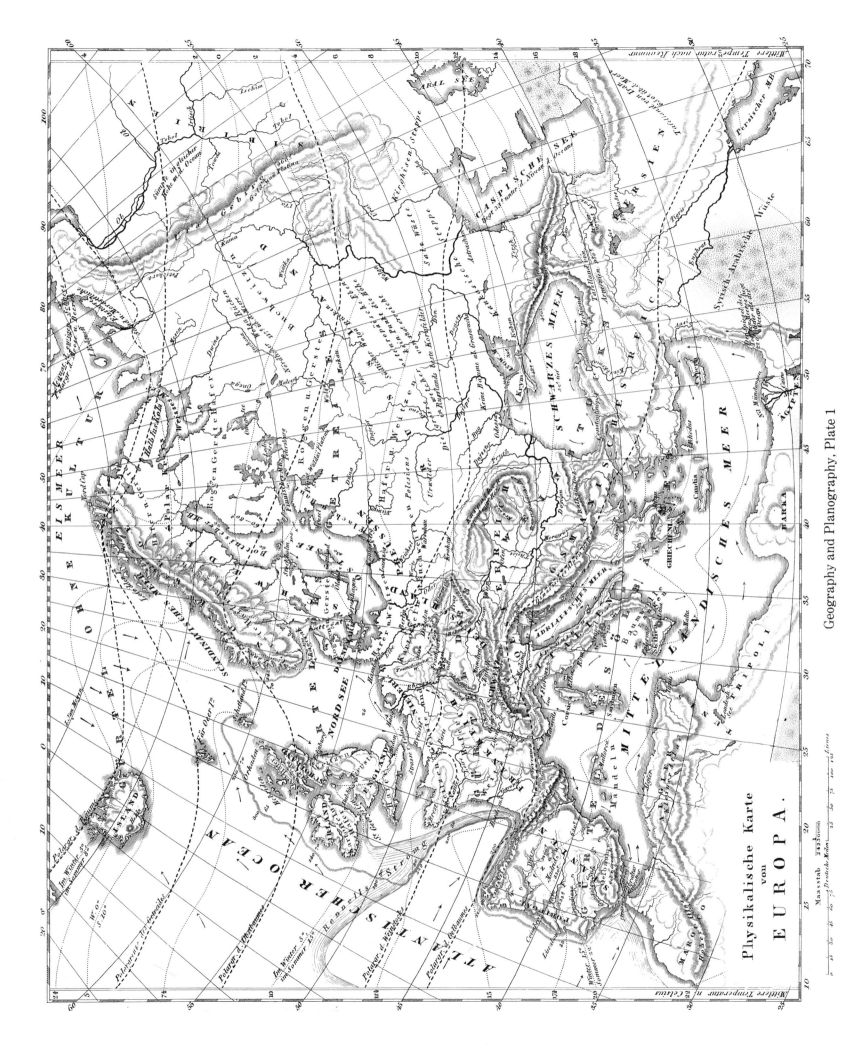

Physikalische Karte
von
EUROPA.

Geography and Planography, Plate 1

1

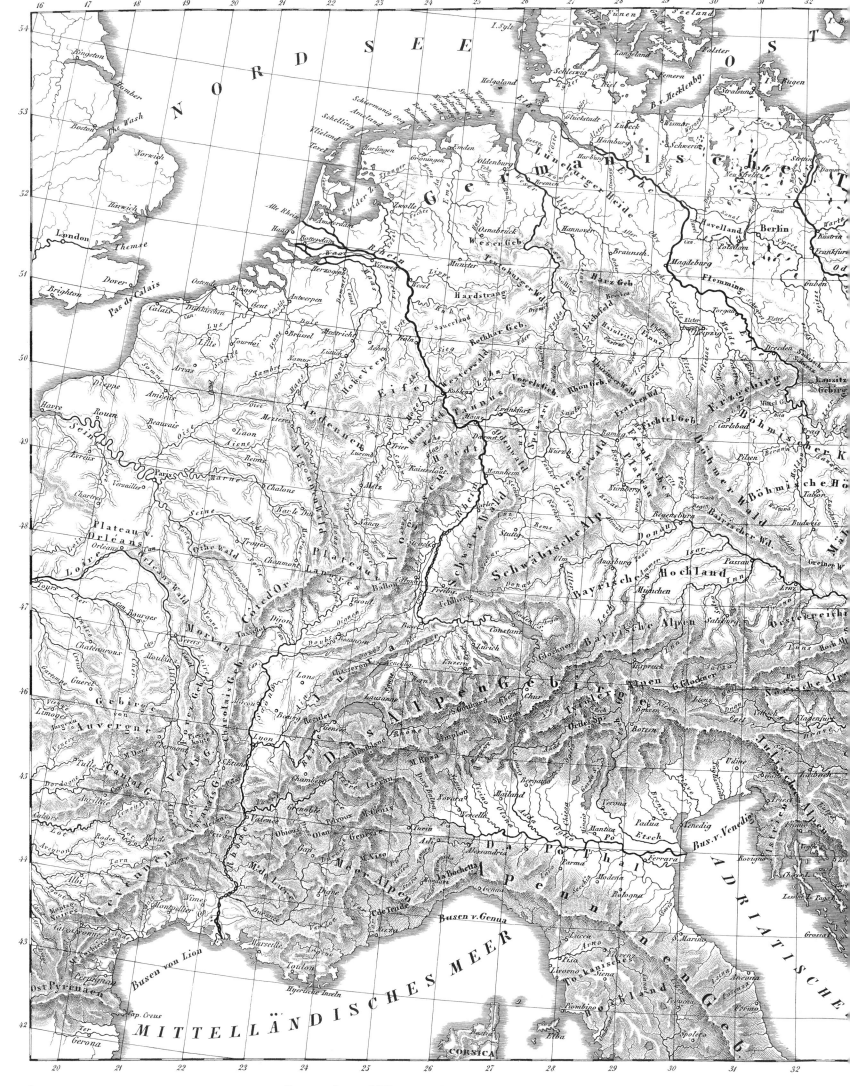

Geography and Planography, Plates 2 and 3

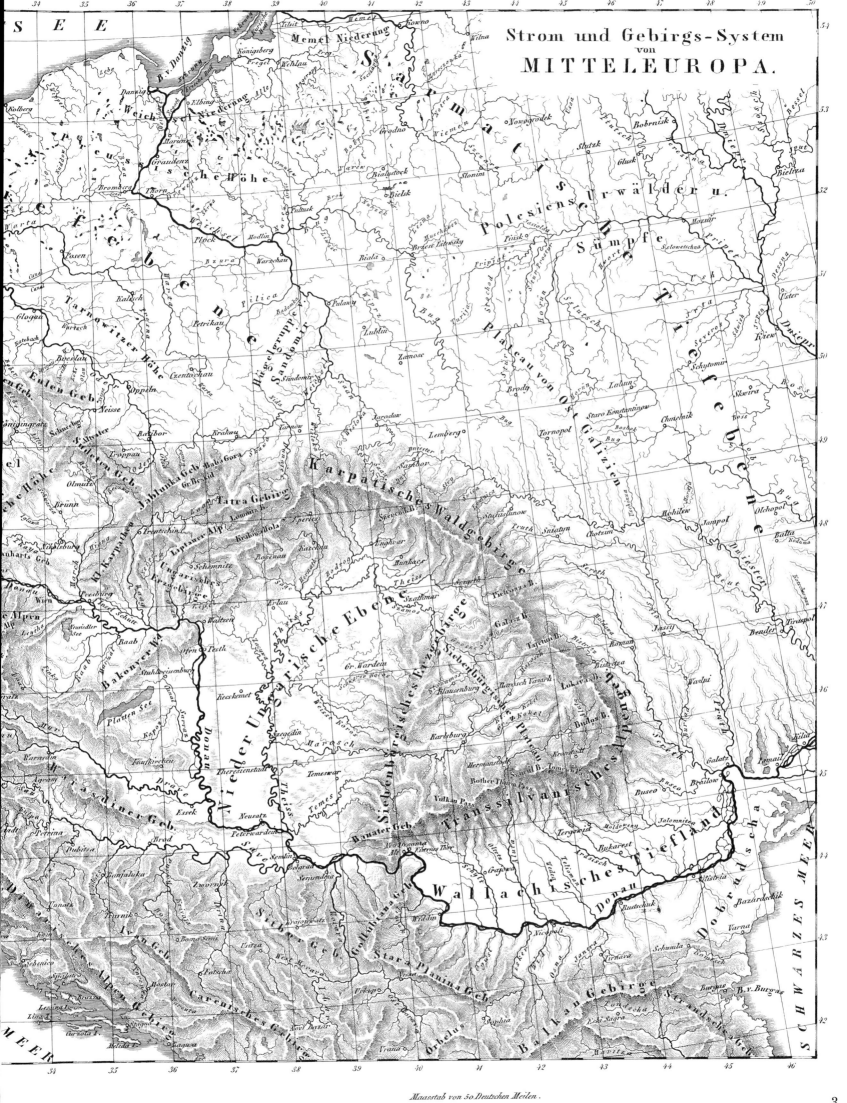

Strom und Gebirgs-System
von
MITTELEUROPA.

Maasstab von 50 Deutschen Meilen.

3

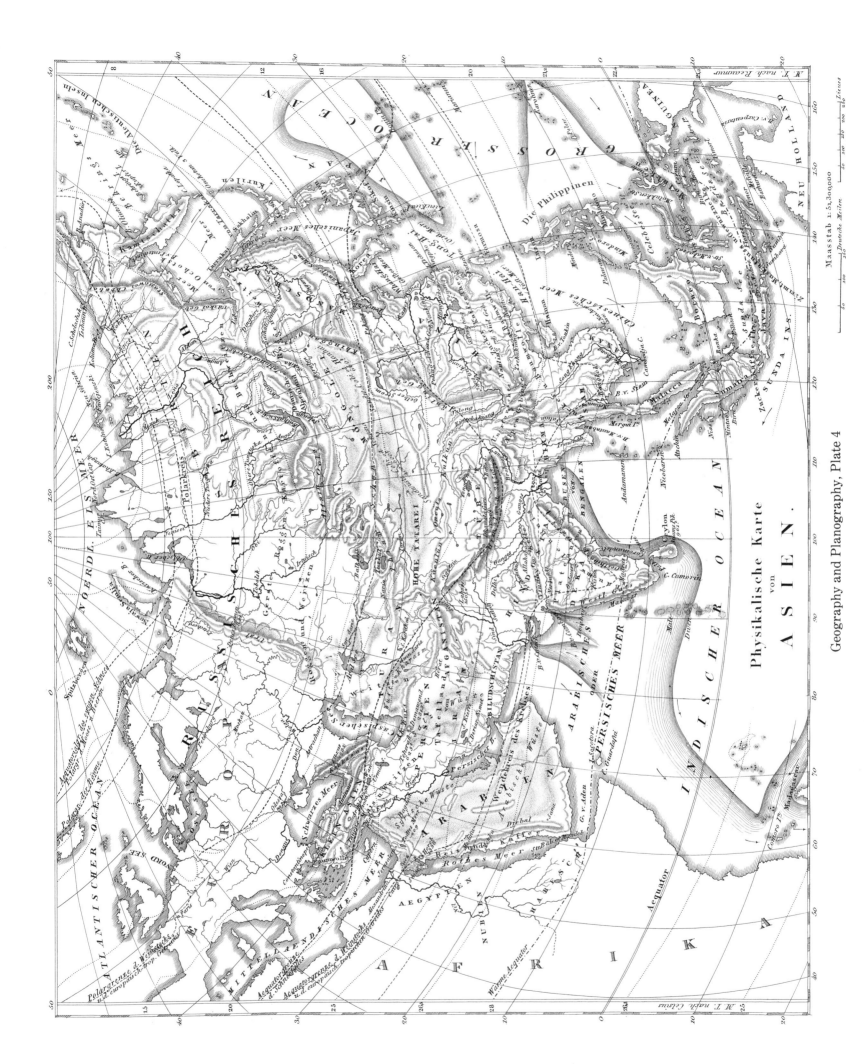

Physikalische Karte
von
ASIEN.

Geography and Planography, Plate 4

Maasstab 1:51,300,000

4

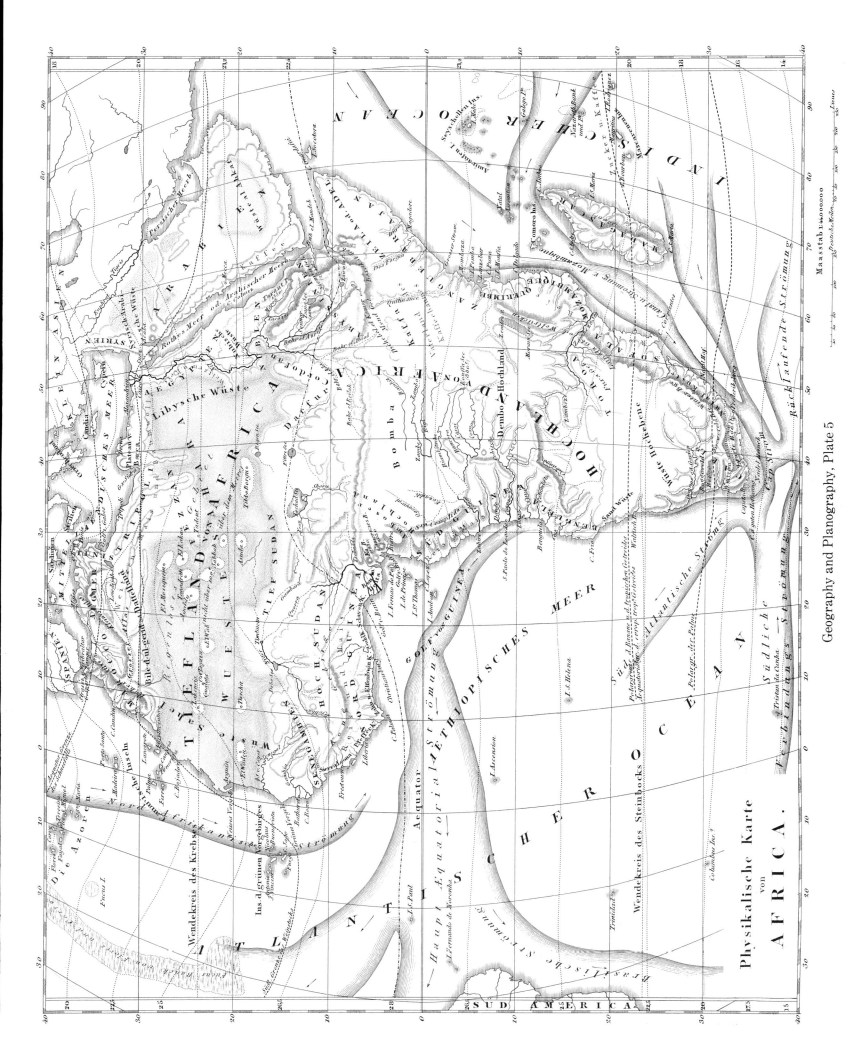

Physikalische Karte
von
AFRICA.

Geography and Planography, Plate 5

5

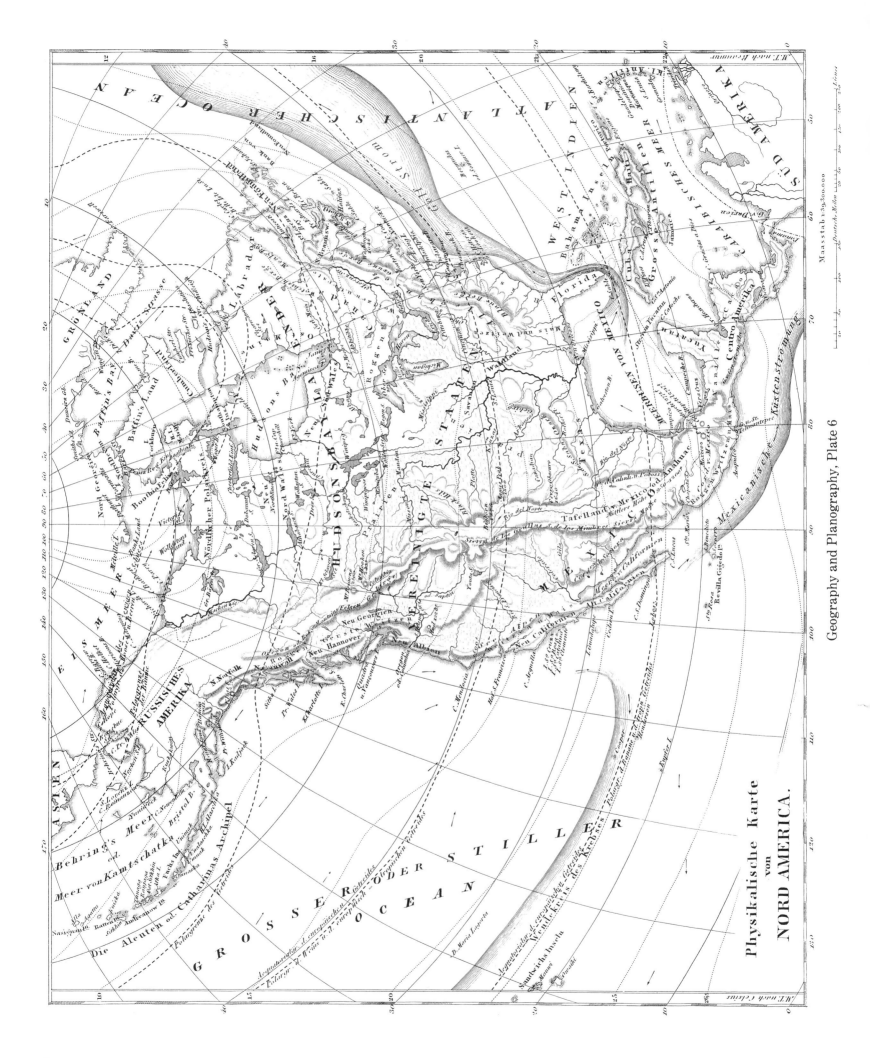

Physikalische Karte
von
NORD AMERICA.

Geography and Planography, Plate 6

6

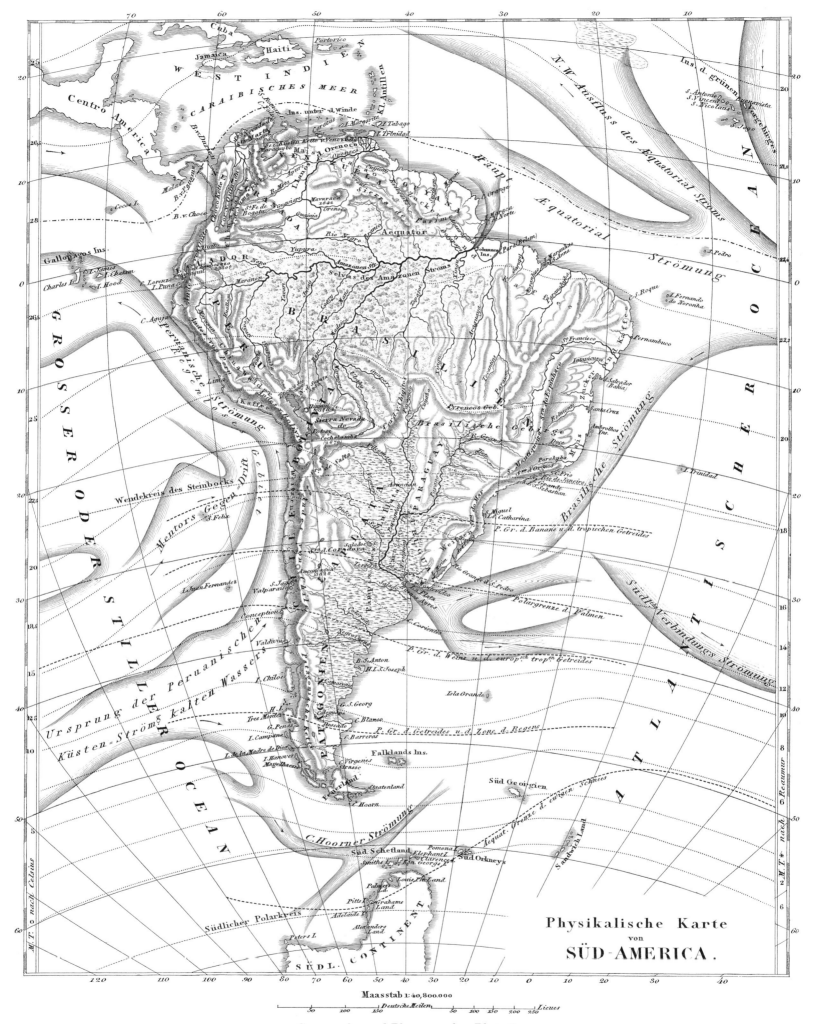

Physikalische Karte
von
SÜD-AMERICA.

Maasstab 1: 40,800.000

Geography and Planography, Plate 7

7

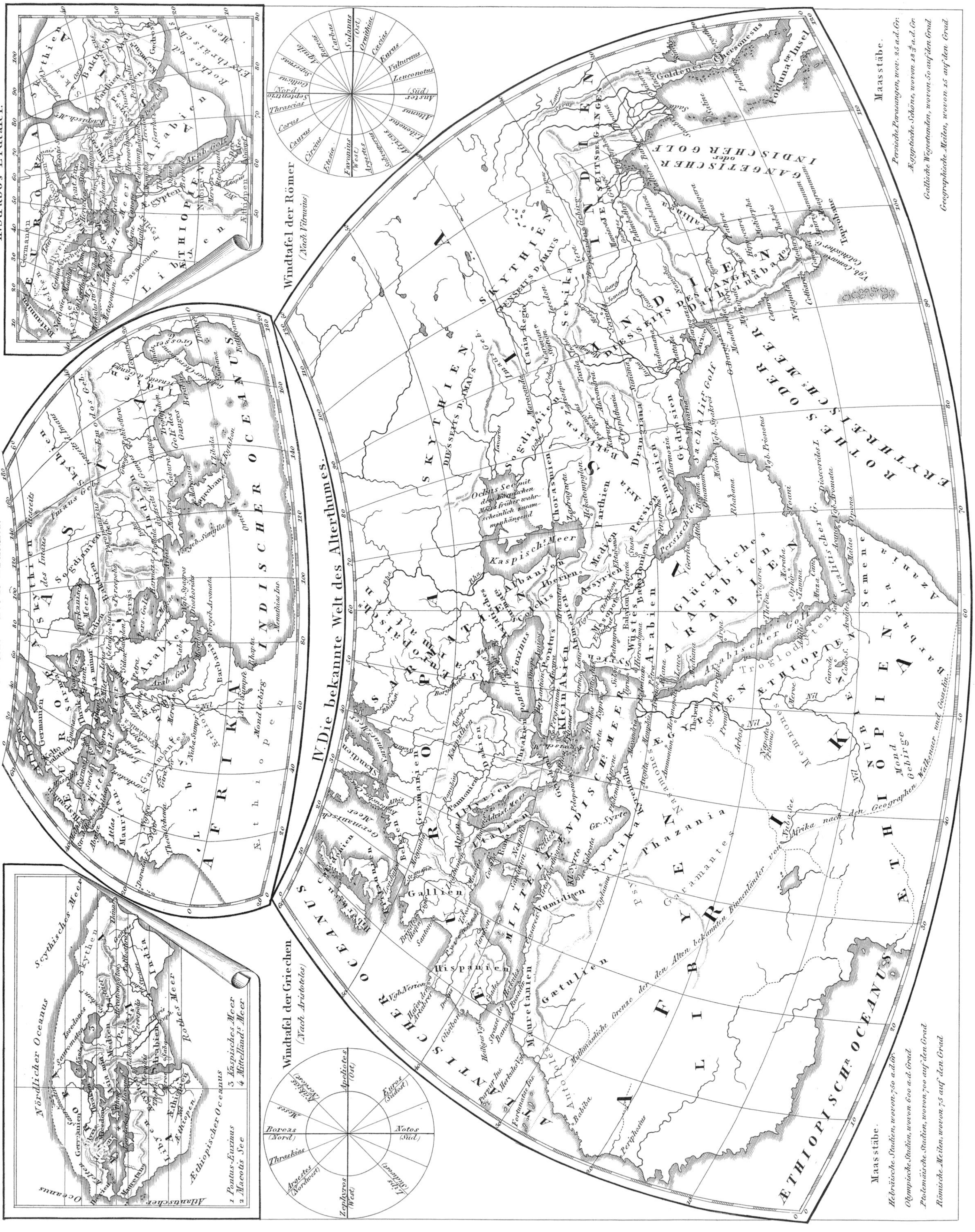

I. Herodots Erdtafel.

II. Strabos Erdtafel.

III. Ptolemäische Erdtafel.

IV. Die bekannte Welt des Alterthumes.

Windtafel der Römer (Nach Vitruvius)

Windtafel der Griechen (Nach Aristoteles)

Boreas (Nord)
Notos (Süd)
Zephyros (West)
Apheliotes (Ost)
Euros (Südost)
Thrasbias
Argestes (Nordwest)

Septentrio (Nord)
Auster (Süd)
Solanus
Favonius

Maasstäbe.
Hebräische Stadien, wovon 530 a.d.Gr.
Olympische Stadien, wovon 600 a.d. Grad.
Ptolemäische Stadien, wovon 700 auf den Grad.
Römische Meilen, wovon 75 auf den Grad.

Maasstabe.
Persische Parasangen, wovon 25 a.d.Gr.
Egyptische Schön, wovon 18 ½ a.d. Gr.
Galliche Wegstunden, wovon 20 auf den Grad.
Geographische Meilen, wovon 15 auf den Grad.

Geography and Planography, Plate 8

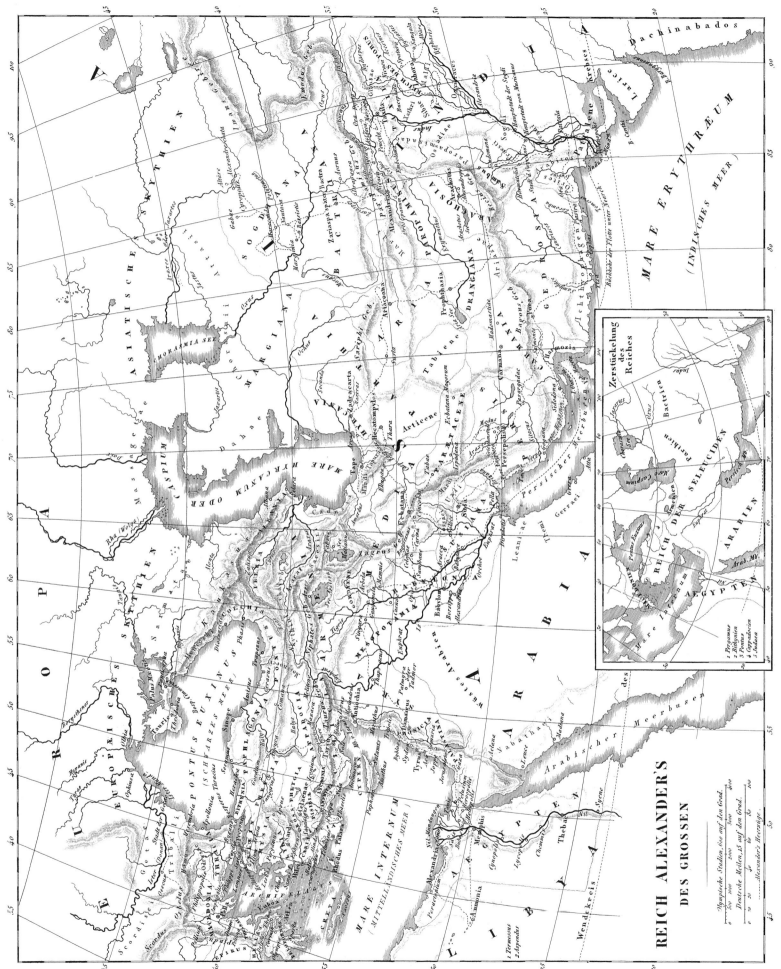

REICH ALEXANDER'S
DES GROSSEN

Zerstückelung
des
Reiches

1 Pergamus
2 Bithynien
3 Pontus
4 Cappadocien
5 Judaea

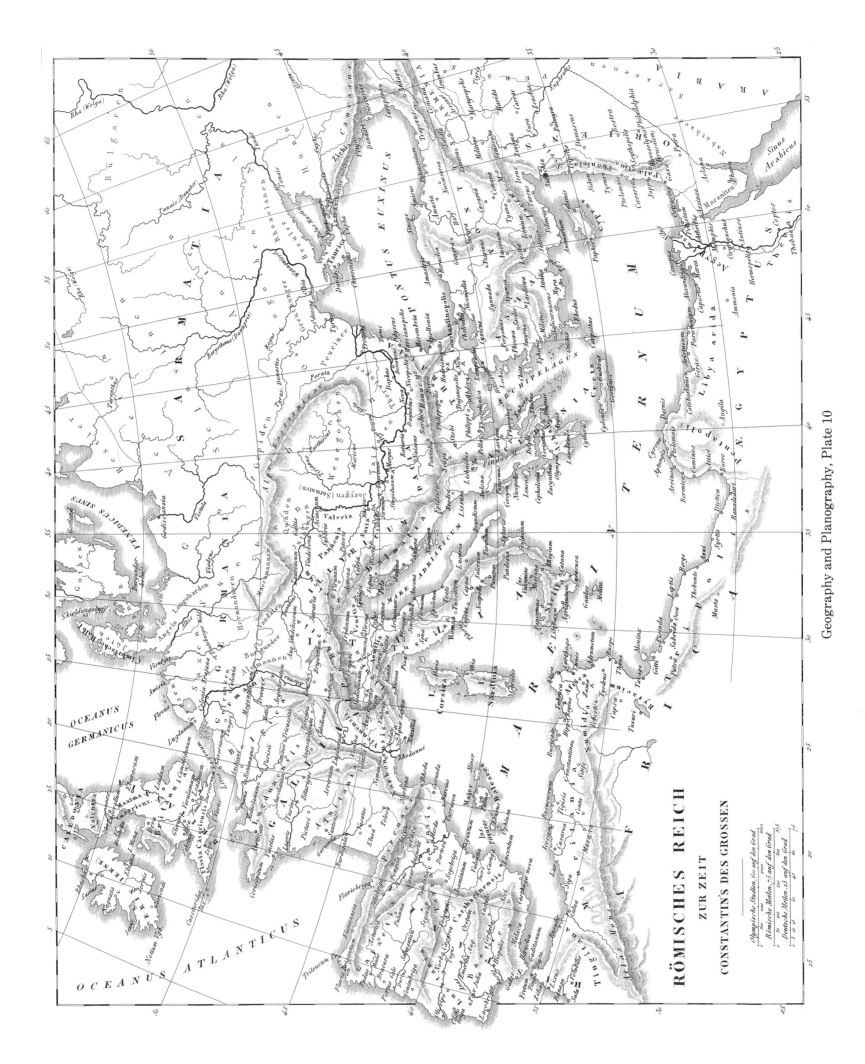

RÖMISCHES REICH

ZUR ZEIT

CONSTANTIN'S DES GROSSEN

Geography and Planography, Plate 10

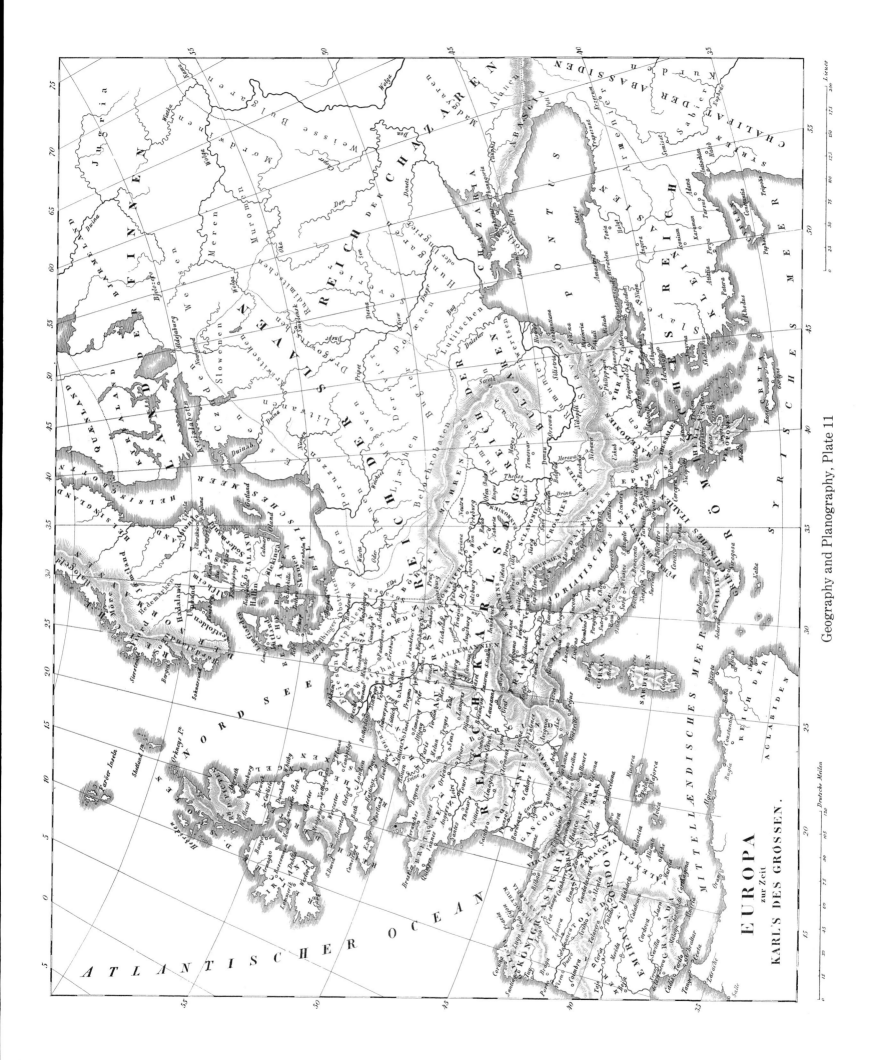

EUROPA
zur Zeit
KARL'S DES GROSSEN.

Geography and Planography, Plate 11

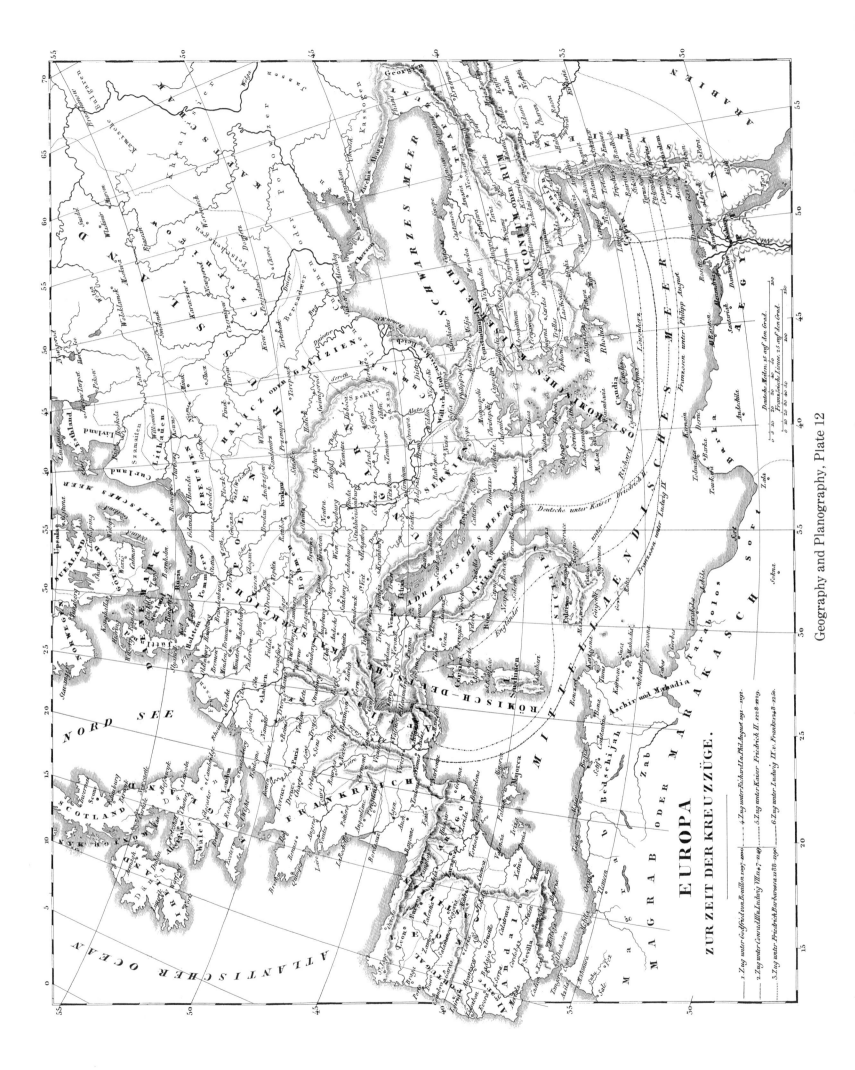

EUROPA
ZUR ZEIT DER KREUZZÜGE.

Geography and Planography, Plate 12

12

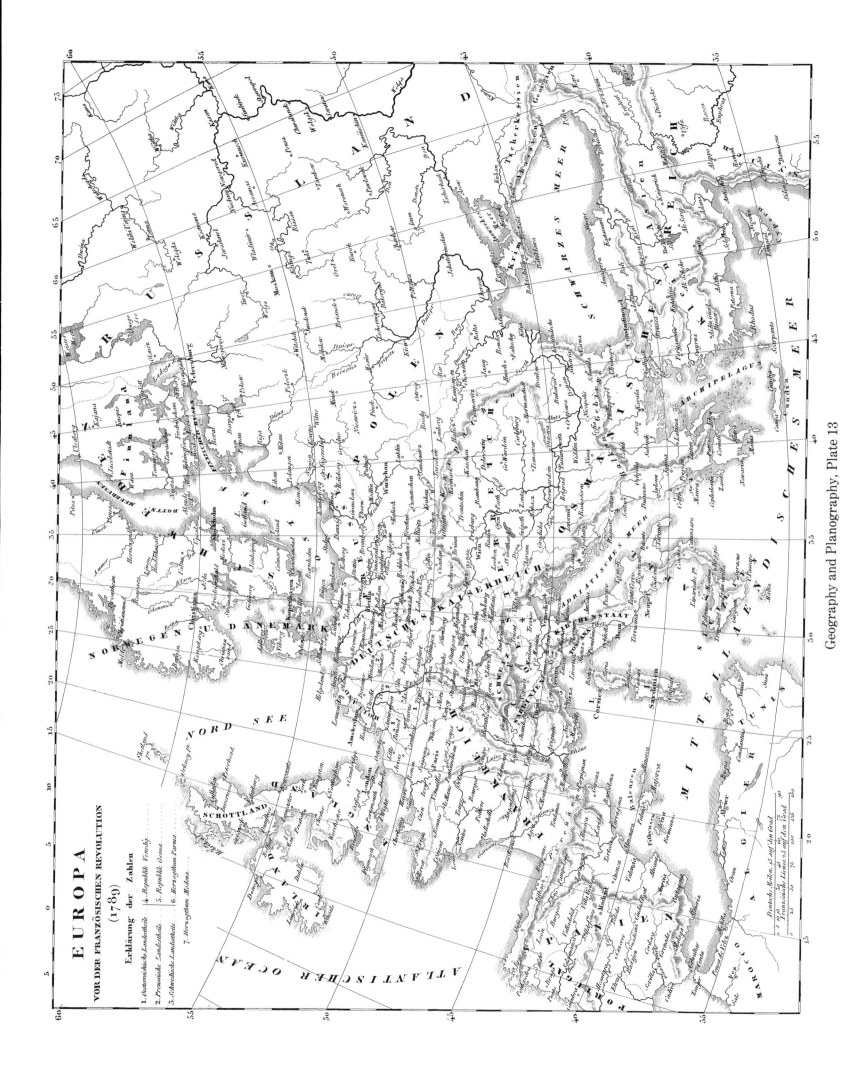

EUROPA
VOR DER FRANZÖSISCHEN REVOLUTION
(1789)

Erklärung der Zahlen

1. Oesterreichische Landestheile ......
2. Preussische Landestheile ......
3. Schwedische Landestheile ......
4. Republik Venedig ......
5. Republik Genua ......
6. Herzogthum Parma ......
7. Herzogthum Modena ......

Geography and Planography, Plate 13

13

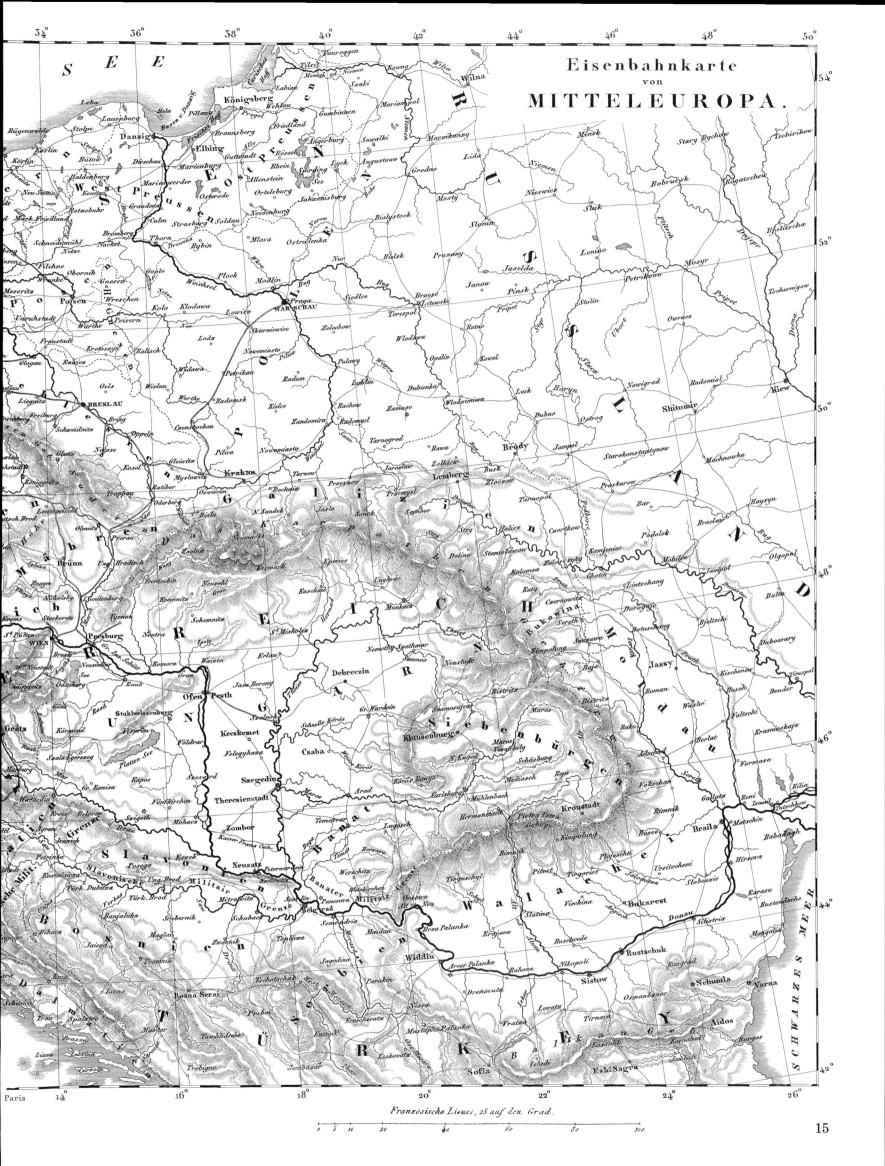

Geography and Planography, Plate 16

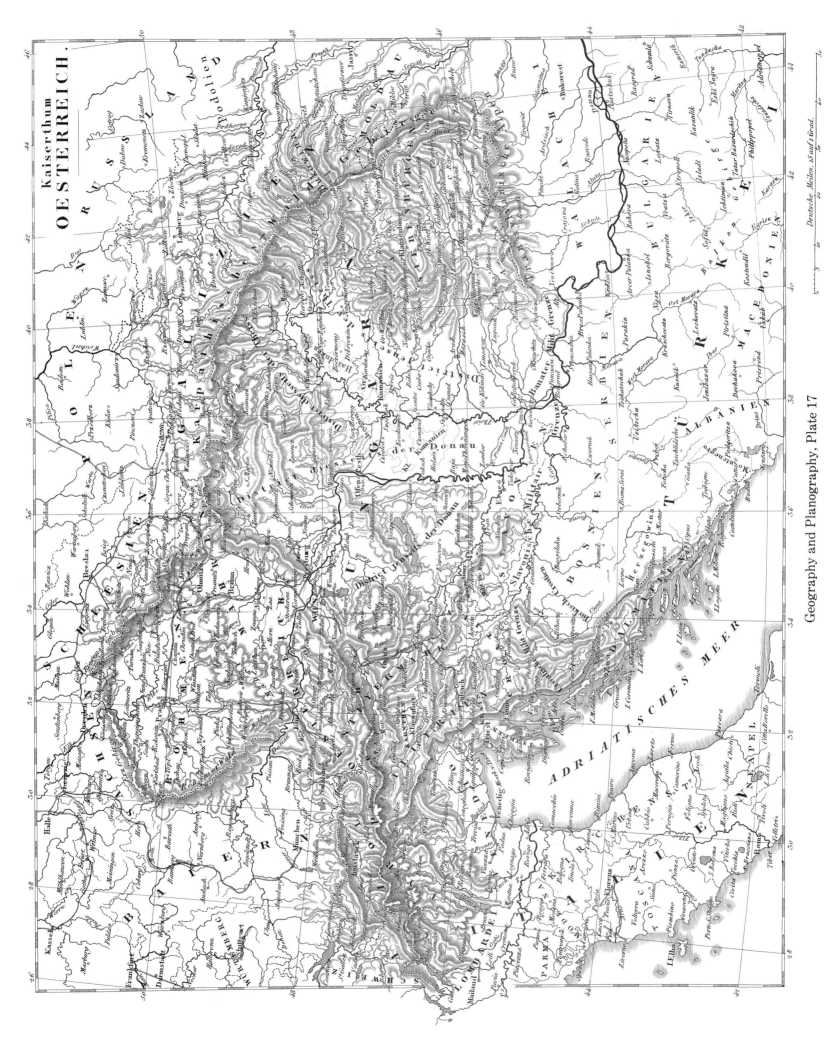

Kaiserthum
OESTERREICH.

ADRIATISCHES MEER

Geography and Planography, Plate 17

17

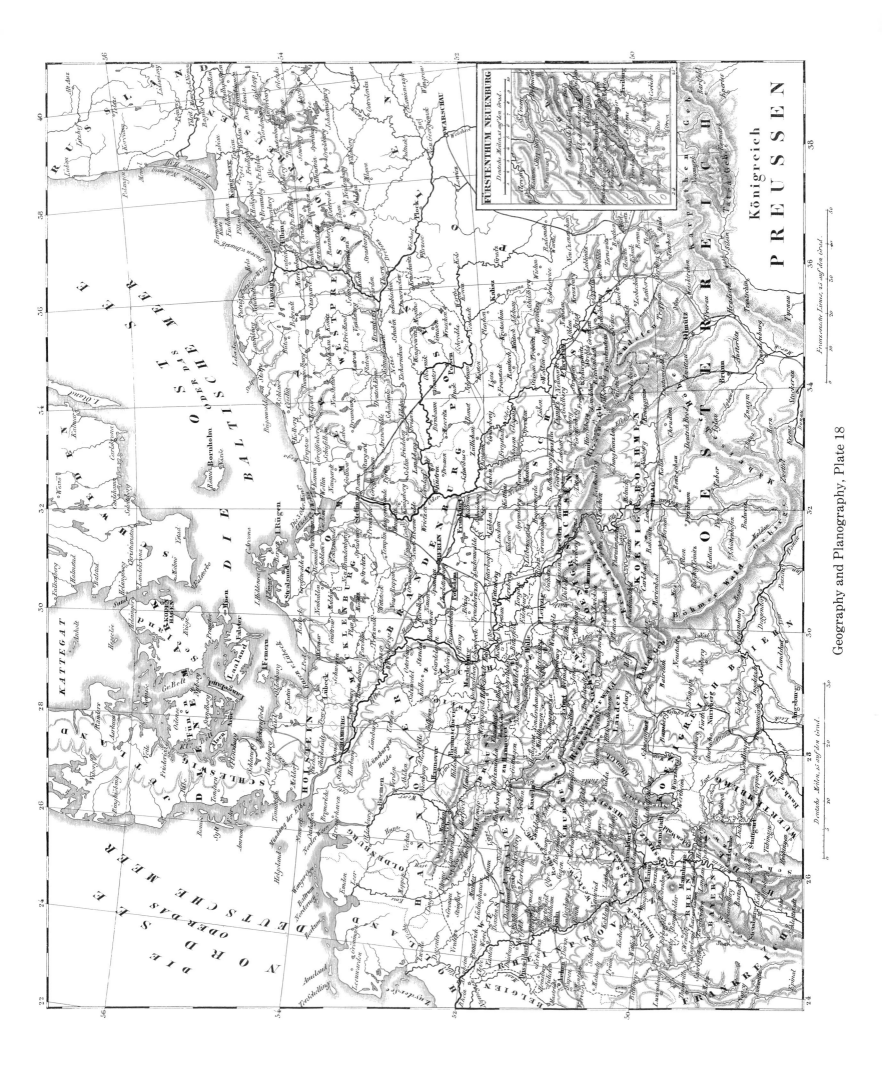

Geography and Planography, Plate 18

18

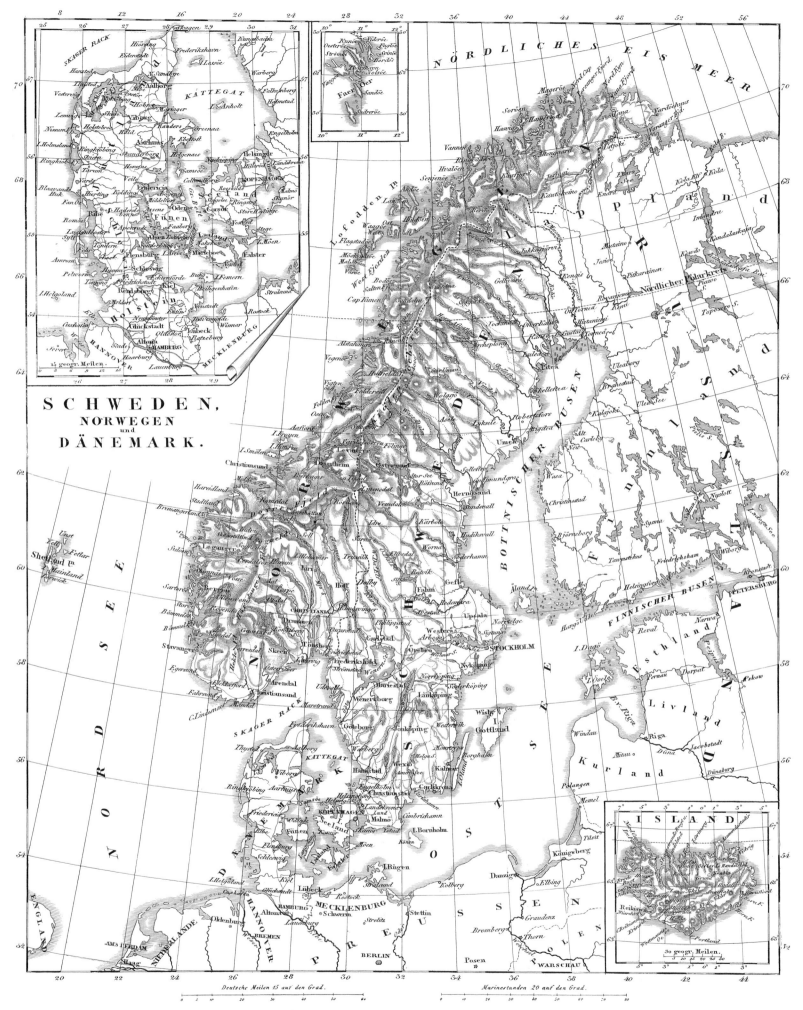

SCHWEDEN,
NORWEGEN
und
DÄNEMARK.

Geography and Planography, Plate 19

19

GROSSBRITANNIEN
und
IRELAND.

Maasstäbe.

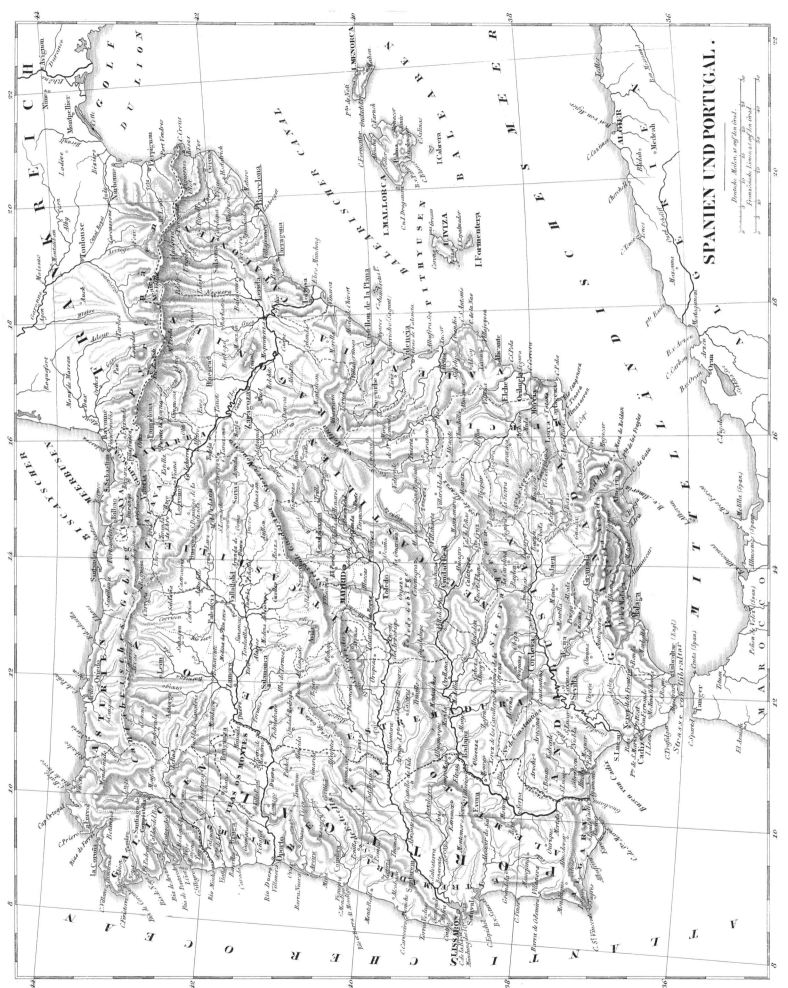

SPANIEN UND PORTUGAL.

Geography and Planography, Plate 21

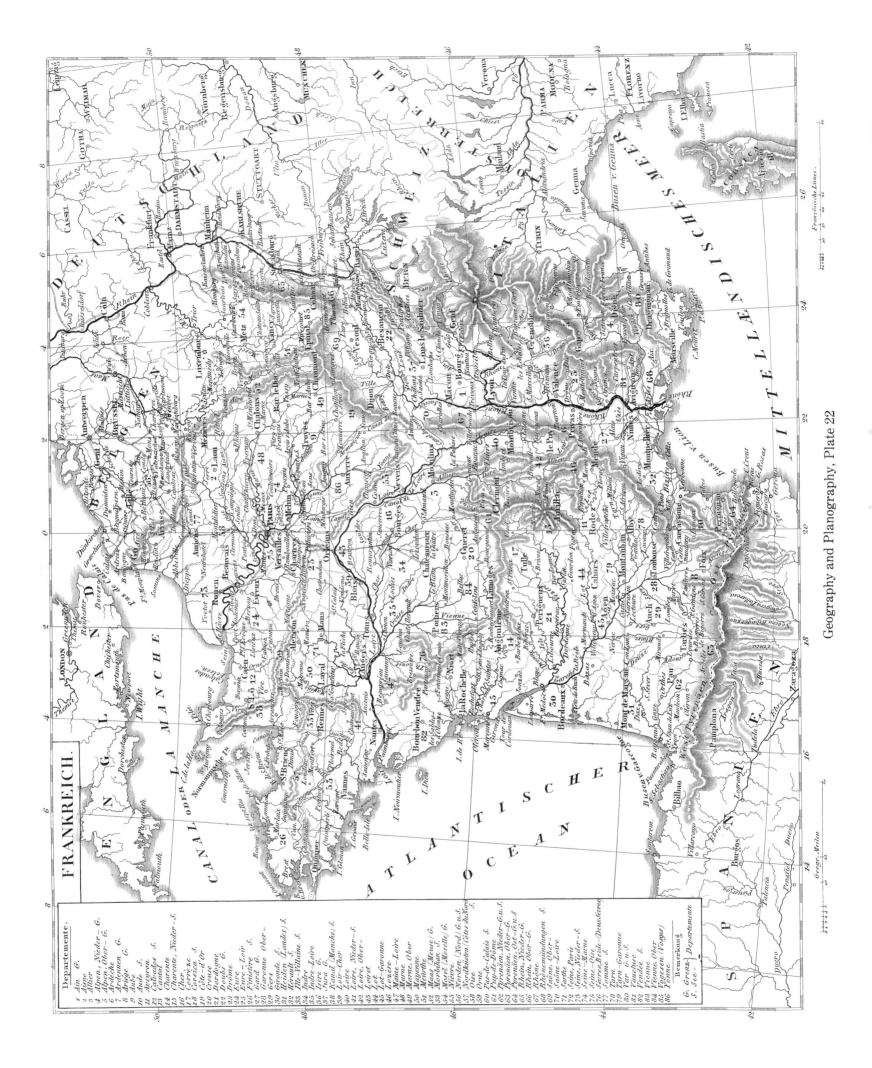

Geography and Planography, Plate 22

22

DIE SCHWEIZ

Nr.	Cantonsnamen	Bevölkerung
1	Zürich	237,460
2	Bern	414,470
3	Luzern	129,500
4	Uri	13,870
5	Schwyz	42,810
6	Unterwalden	23,470
7	Glarus	30,270
8	Zug	15,040
9	Freiburg	94,530
10	Solothurn	63,660
11	Basel, Stadt	23,300
12	Basel, Landschaft	42,730

Nr.	Cantonsnamen	Bevölkerung
13	Schaffhausen	31,990
14	Appenzell	55,480
15	S. Gallen	165,190
16	Graubünden	90,280
17	Aargau	139,080
18	Thurgau	85,490
19	Tessin	111,180
20	Waat	189,310
21	Wallis	75,310
22	Neuenburg	66,500
23	Genf	42,750
	Die ganze Schweiz	2,185,470

Französische Lieues, 25 auf den Grad.

Deutsche Meilen, 15 auf den Grad.

Geography and Planography, Plate 23

ITALIEN.

Maasstäbe

Französische Lieues

Deutsche Meilen

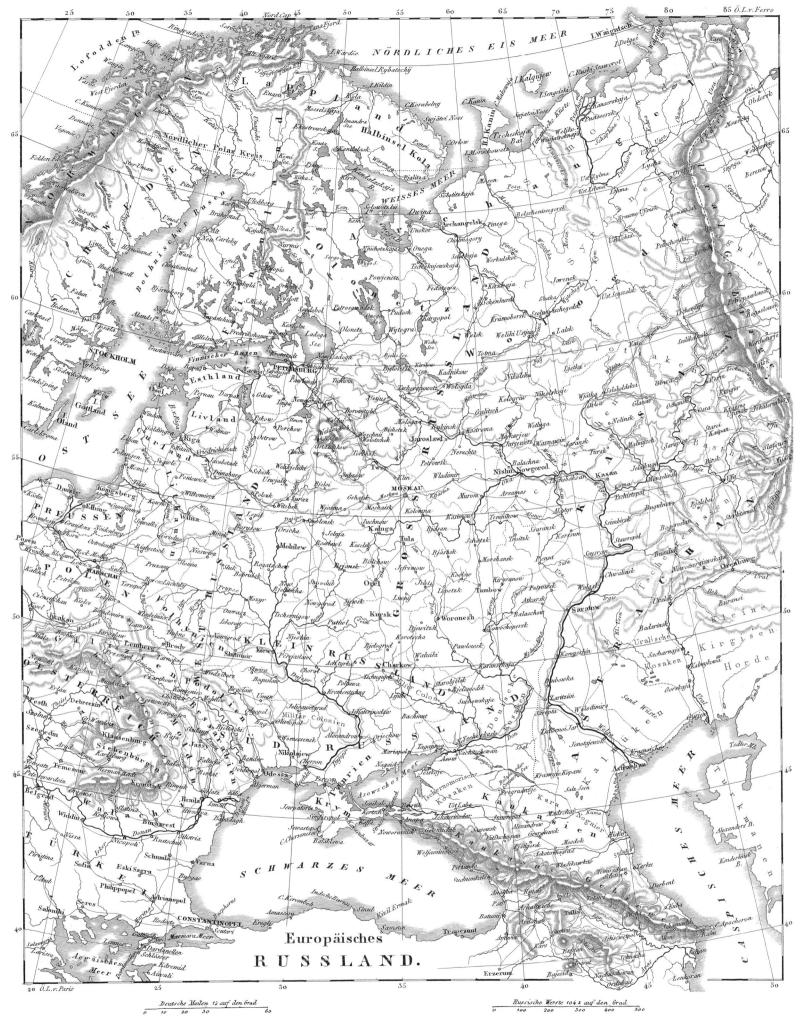

Europäisches
RUSSLAND.

Geography and Planography, Plate 25

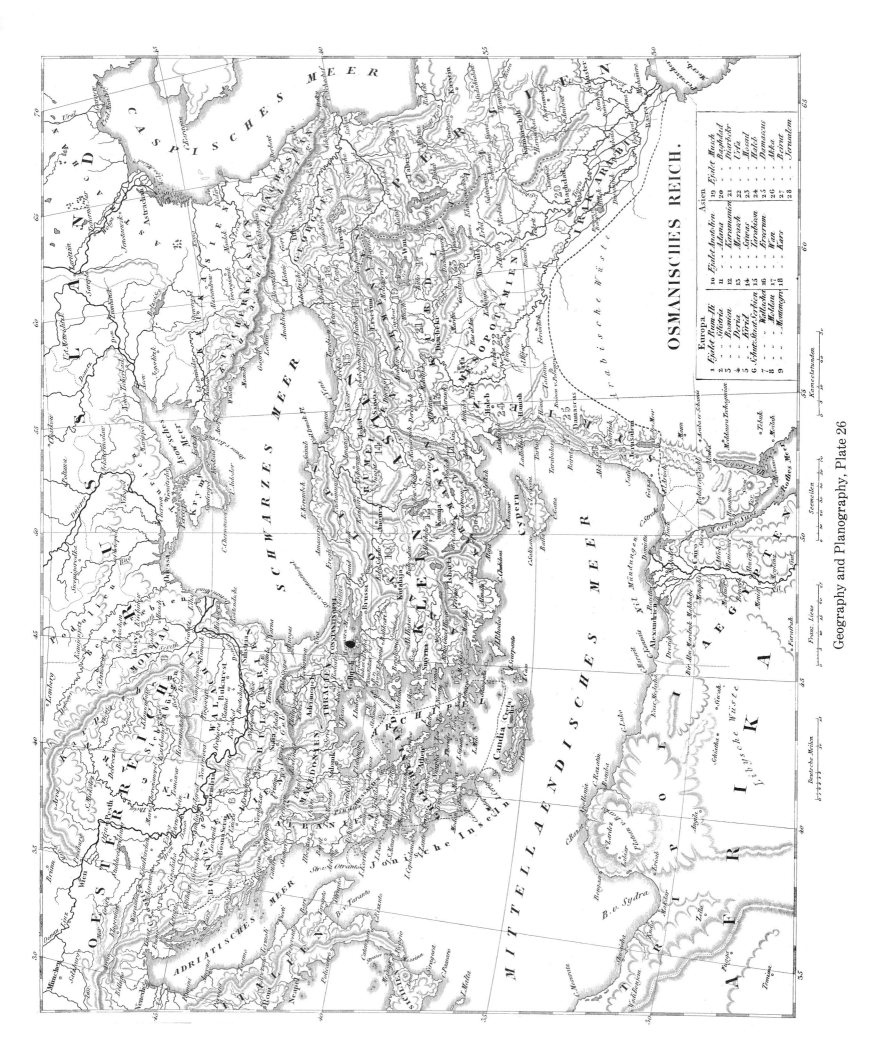

Geography and Planography, Plate 26

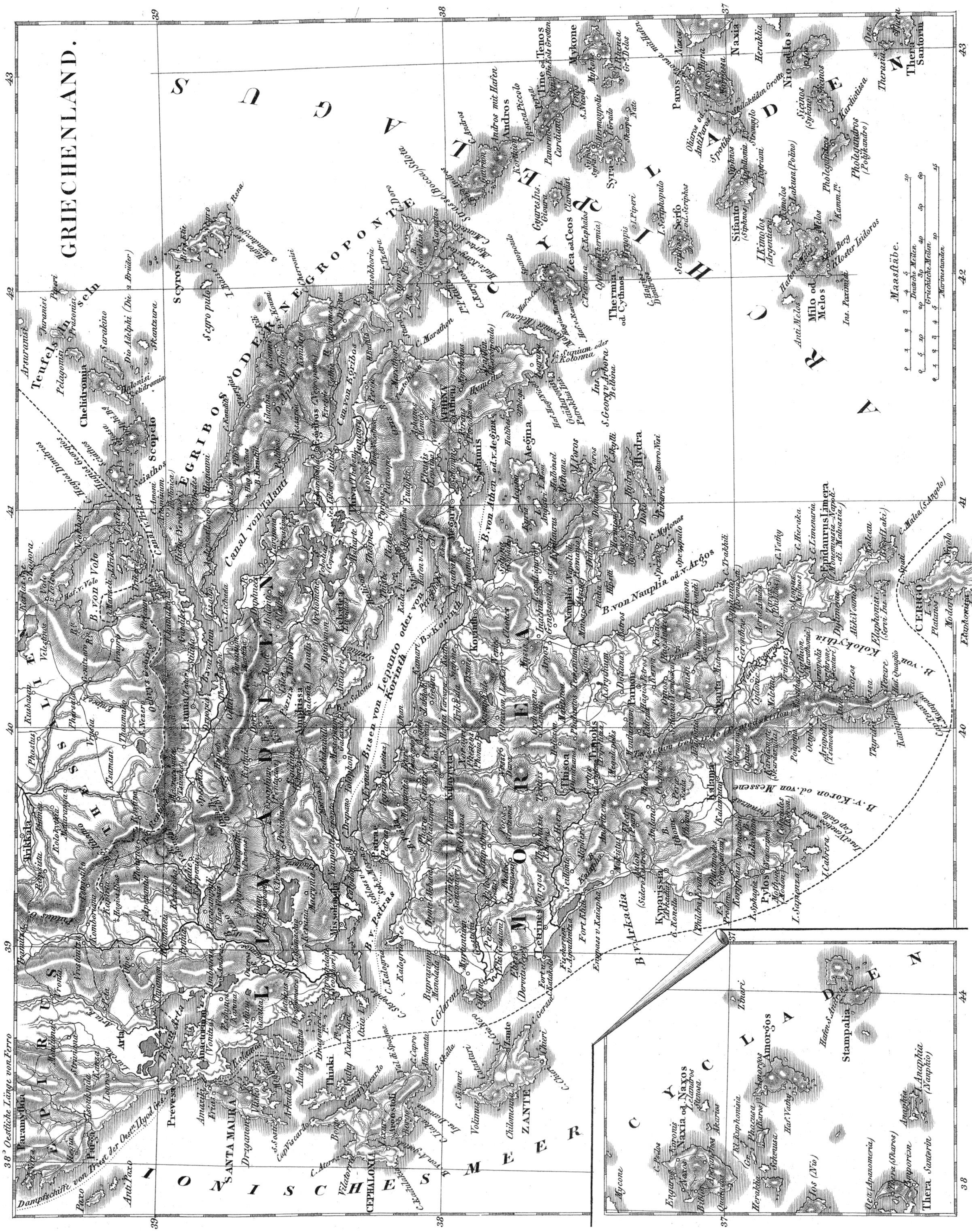

Geography and Planography, Plate 27

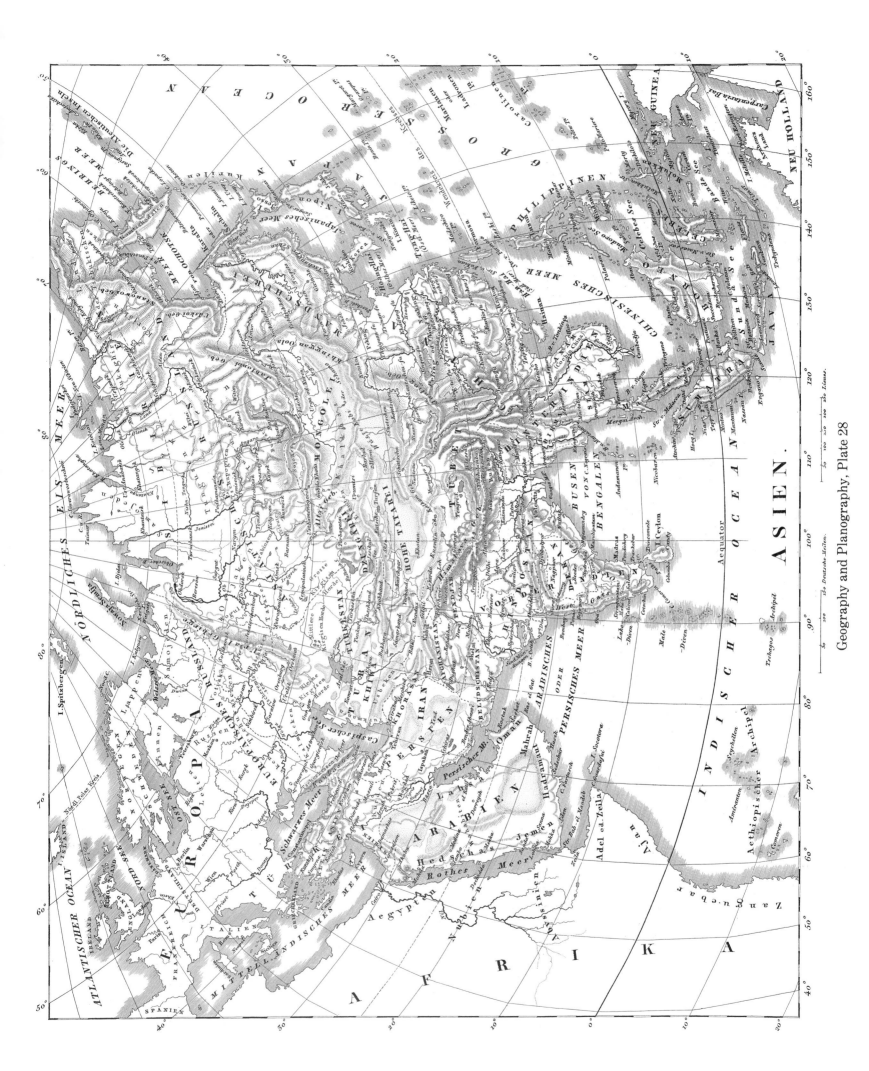

ASIEN.

Geography and Planography, Plate 28

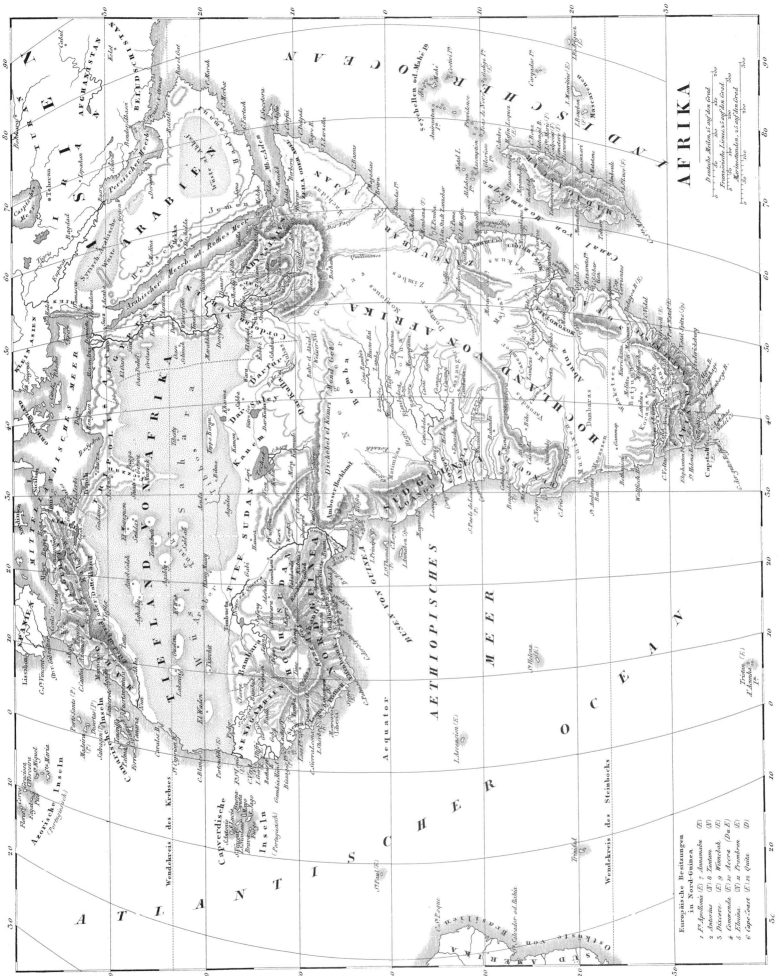

Geography and Planography, Plate 29

NORDAMERICA.

Staaten der Nordamericani-
schen Union

Maine	1	
Newhampshire	2	
Vermont	3	
Massachusetts	4	
Rhode-Island	5	
Connecticut	6	
New York	7	
New-Jersey	8	
Pensylvanien	9	
Delaware	10	
Maryland	11	
Virginien	12	
Nord-Carolina	13	
Süd-Carolina	14	
Georgia	15	
Florida	16	
Alabama	17	
Mississippi	18	

Louisiana 19
Tenessee 20
Kentucky 21
Ohio 22
Indiana 23
Illinois 24
Michigan 25
Missouri 26
Arkansas 27
Wisconsin 28
Iowa 29
Texas 30
Districte.
Distr.Columbia 31
Mandan 33
Ozark 34
Oregon 32

Staaten der Mexicani-
schen Union

Mexico mit dem
Bundesdistrict 1
Queretaro 2
Guanaxuato 3
Mechoacan 4
Xalisco 5
Zacatecas 6
Sonora und 7
Cinaloa
Chihuahua 8
mit Bolson
de Mapimi
Durango 9

La Puebla
mit dem
Distr.Tlascala 16
Oaxaca 17
Chiapa 18
Tabasco 19
Colima 21
Neu-Leon 20
San Luis Potosi 15
Cohahuila 10
Tamaulipas 11
Vera Cruz 12
Californien 20
Neu Mexico 21
Unionsgebiete 19

UMGEBUNG VON NEUYORK

Brasilien 18 Prov.		N. Granada 5 Dep.ts		Bolivia 10 Dep.ts		Valdivia . . . 7
Rio Janeiro	1	Candinamarca	1	Arequipa	1	Insel Chiloe . 8
San Paulo	2	Cauca	2	Ayacucho	2	La Plata 14 Staaten
Sta Catarina	3	Istmo	3	Cusco	3	Buenos Ayres 1
San Pedro	4	Magdalena	4	Puno	4	Entre Rios 2
Matto Grosso	5	Boyaca	5	Chuquisaqua	5	Corrientes 3
Goyaz	6	Venezuela 4 Dep.ts		Oruro	6	Sta Fé 4
Minas Geraes	7	Venezuela	1	Potosi	7	Cordova 5
Espirito Santo	8	Maturin	2	La Paz	8	Santiago 6
Bahia	9	Orenoco	3	Cochabamba	9	Tucuman 7
Sergipe del Rey	10	Zulia	4	Sta Cruz und 10		Salta 8
Dos Alagoas	11	Ecuador 3 Dep.ts		Provins Tarija 11		Juguy 9
Pernambuco	12	Ecuador	1	Chile 8 Provinzen		Catamarca 10
Parahyba	13	Guayaquil	2	San Jago	1	Rieja 11
Rio grande	14	Assuay	3	Coquimbo	2	San Juan 12
Ceara	15	Peru 3 Depart.s		Coquimbo	3	San Luis 13
Piauhy	16	Lima	1	Colchagua	4	Mendoza 14
Maranhao	17	Libertad	2	Maule	5	Paraguay
Para	18	Junin	3	Conception	6	Uruguay

SÜDAMERICA

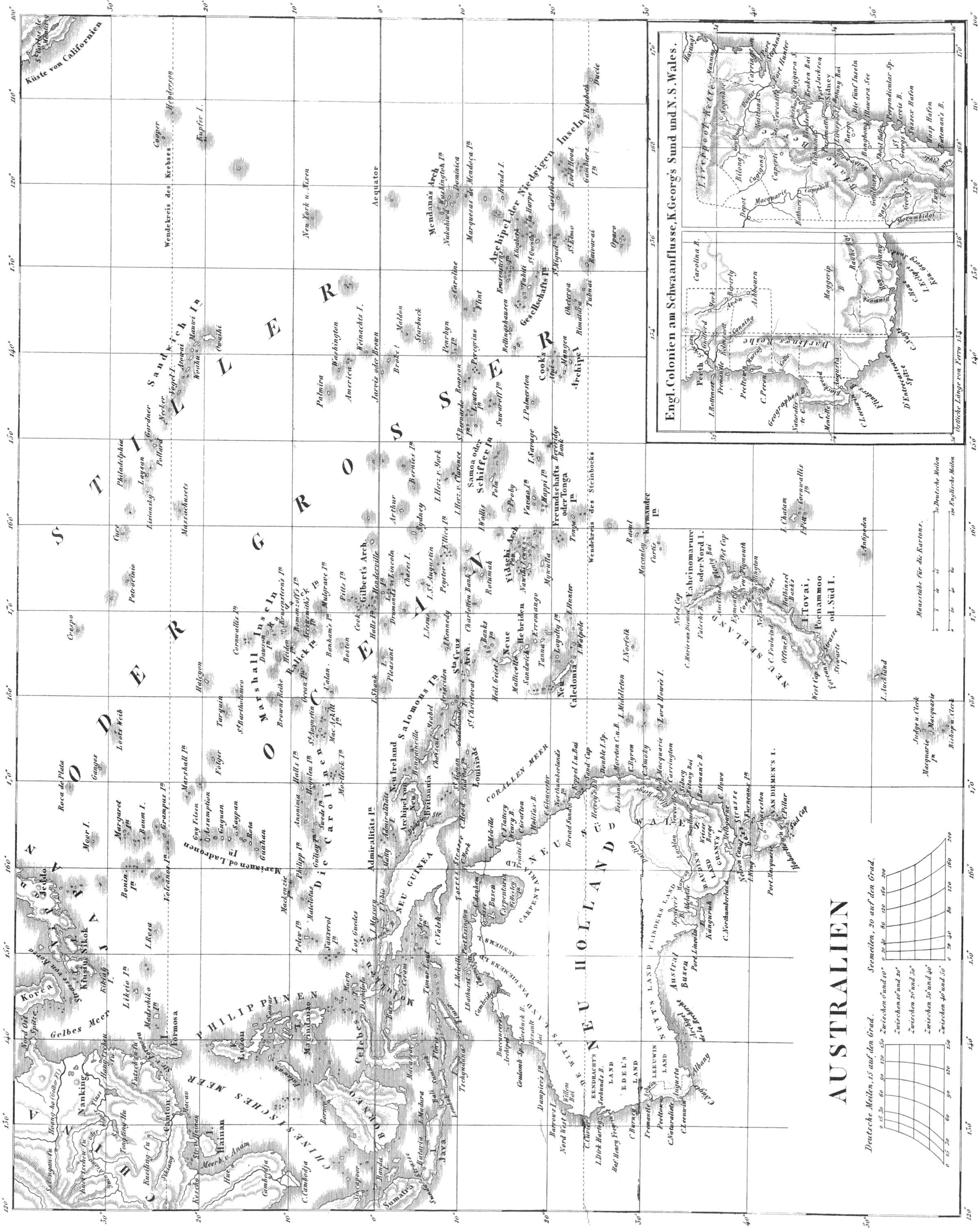

AUSTRALIEN

Geography and Planography, Plate 32

STILLER ODER GROSSER OCEAN

Küste von Californien

Sandwich Is.

Wendekreis des Krebses

Aequator

Wendekreis des Steinbocks

Marshall Inseln

Die Carolinen

Marianen od. Ladronen

Gilbert's Arch.

Mendana's Arch.

Archipel der Niedrigen Inseln

Gesellschafts In.

Marquesas de Mendoza

Samoa oder Schiffer In.

Freundschafts oder Tonga In.

Fidschi Arch.

Neue Hebriden

Neu Caledonia

Salomons In.

New Ireland

Admiralitäts In.

NEU GUINEA

CORALLEN MEER

NEU HOLLAND

N. S. WALES

VAN DIEMEN'S I.

NEU SEELAND

CARPENTARIA

ARNHEIMS LAND

NUYTS LAND

EDELS LAND

LEEUWIN LAND

CHINESISCHES MEER

PHILIPPINEN

Celebes Meer

Borneo

Java

Sumatra

Gelbes Meer

Korea

Formosa

Hainan

Nankin

Maassstab für die Kartons.

Deutsche Meilen, 15 auf den Grad.

Seemeilen, 20 auf den Grad.

Engl. Colonien am Schwaanflusse, K.Georg's Sund und N.S.Wales.

Perth

Port Jackson

Darling's Küste

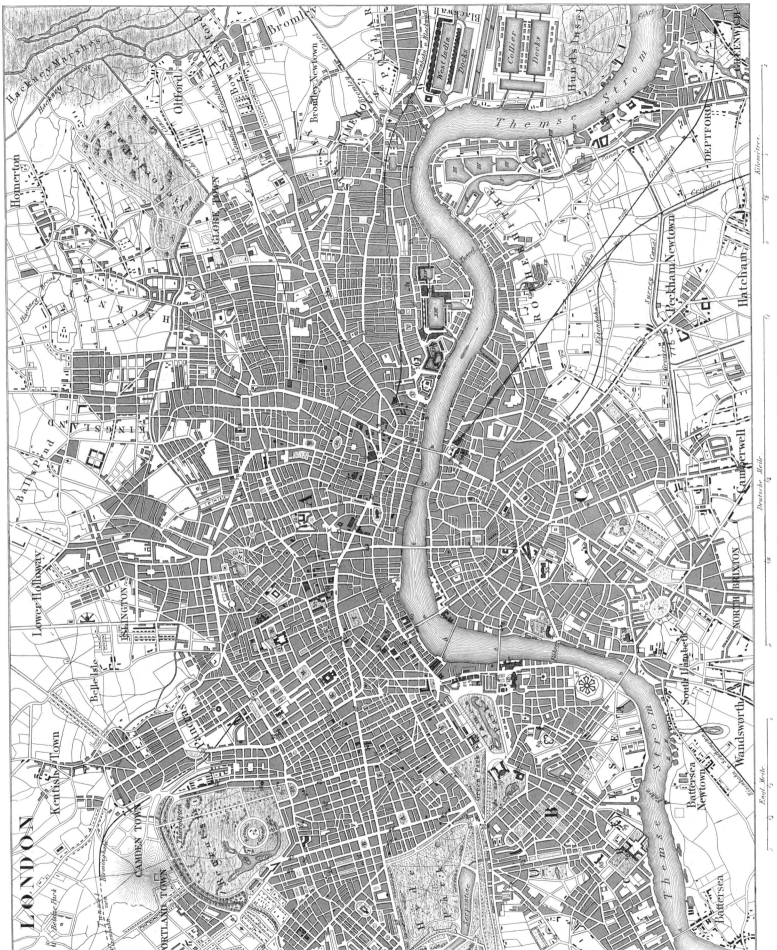

Geography and Planography, Plate 33

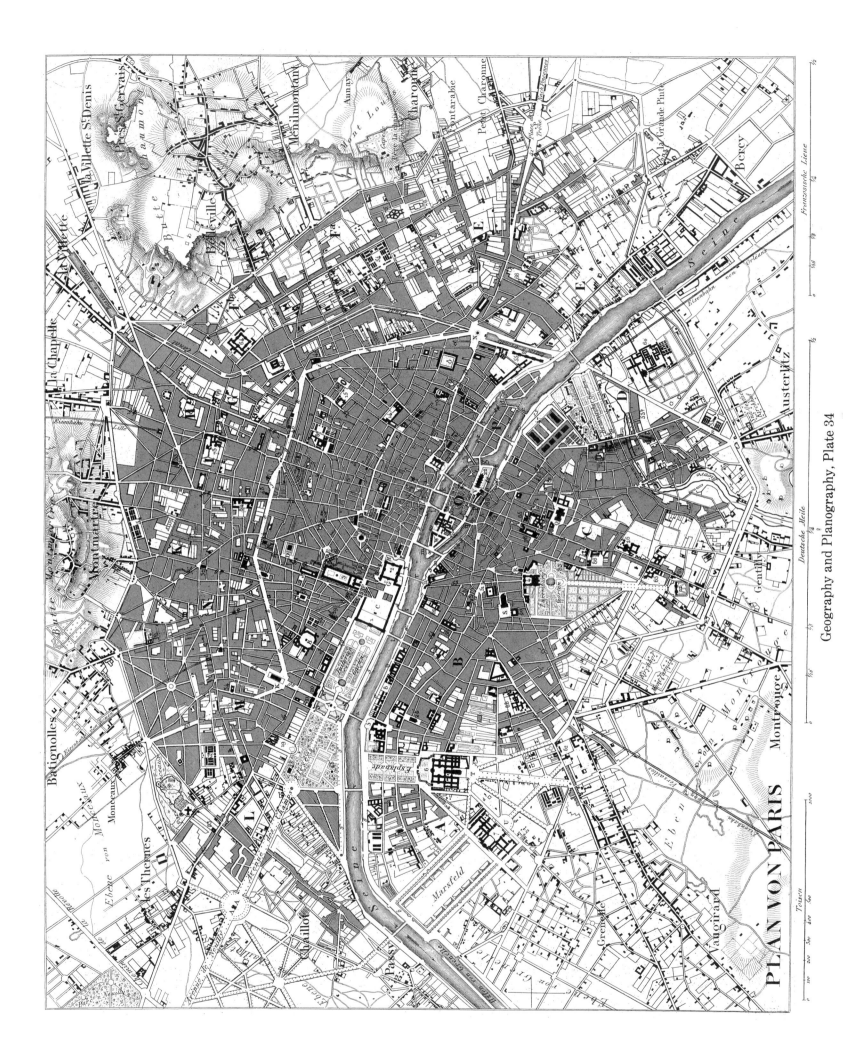

PLAN VON PARIS

Geography and Planography, Plate 34

34

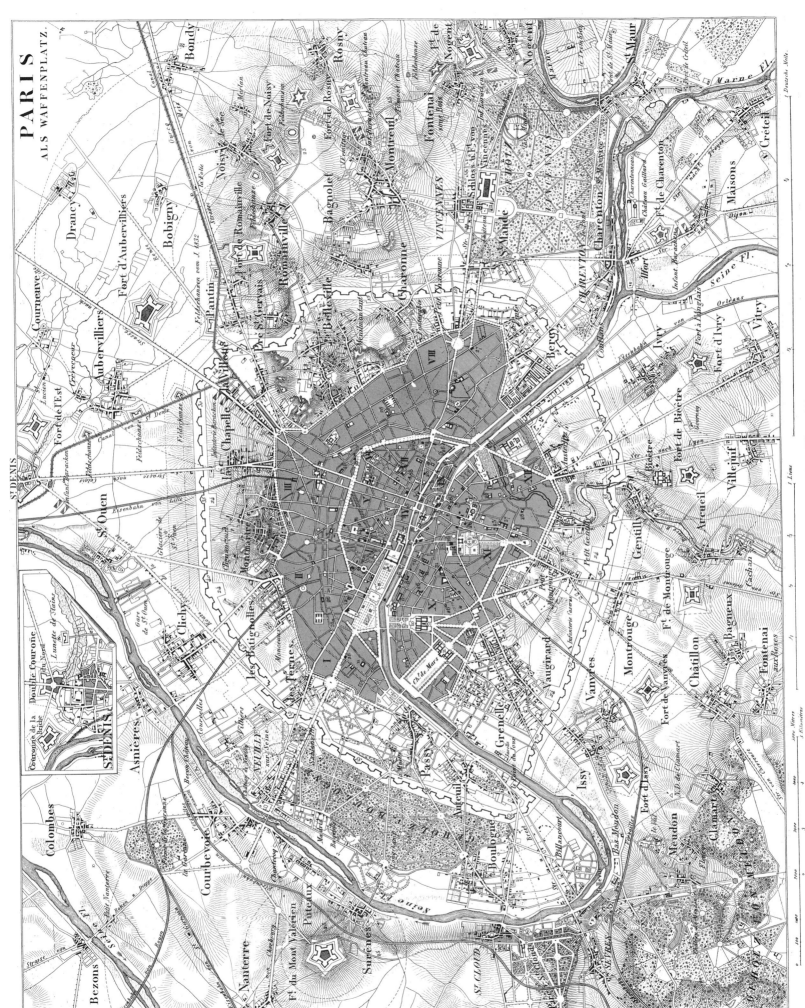

PARIS
ALS WAFFENPLATZ.

Geography and Planography, Plate 35

35

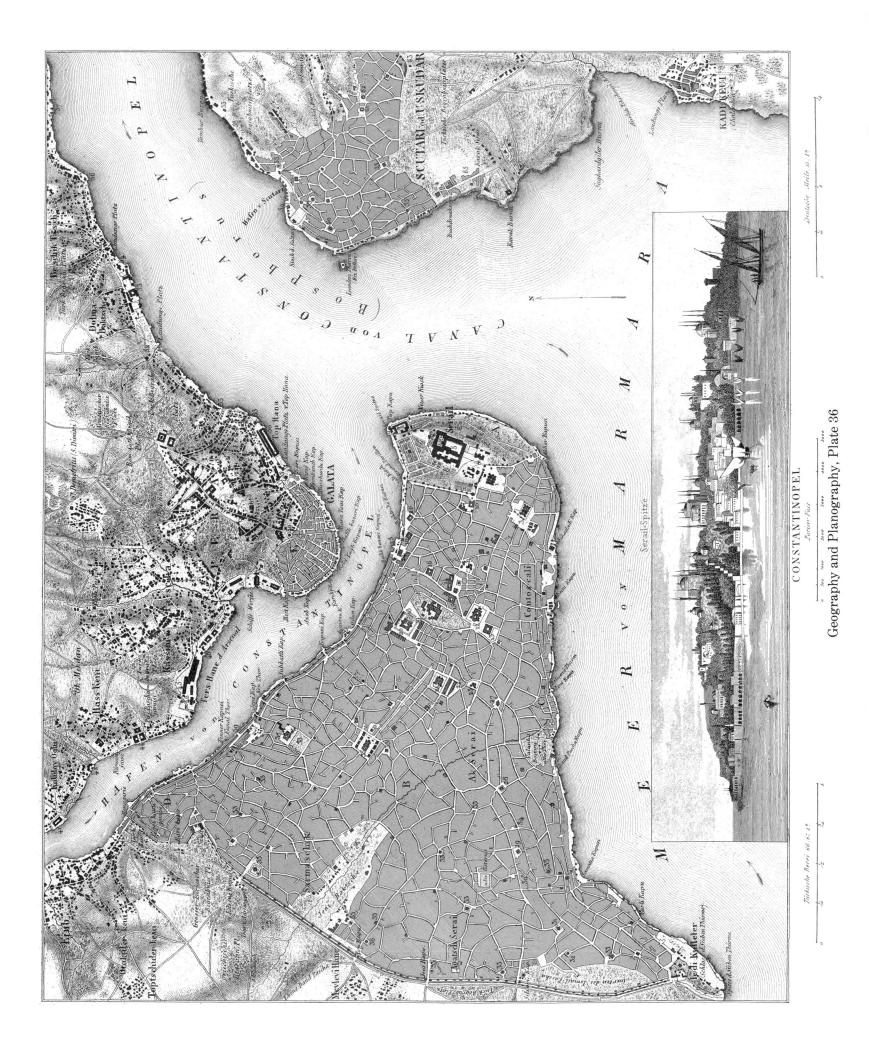

CONSTANTINOPEL
Pariser Fuss

Geography and Planography, Plate 36

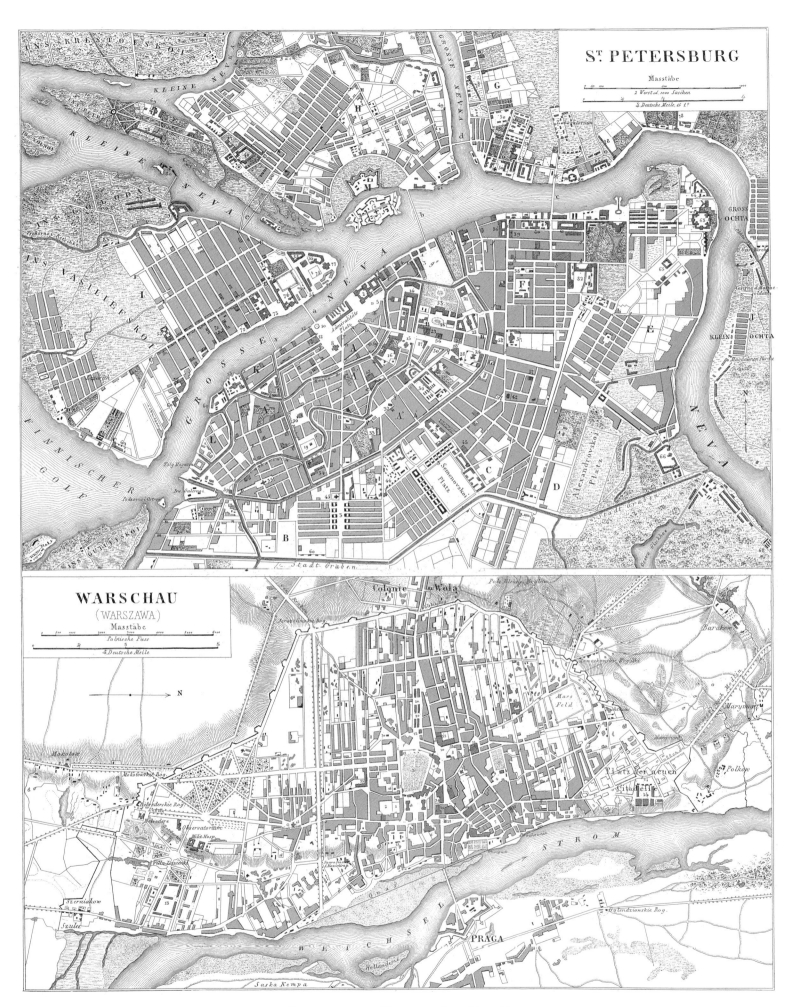

ST. PETERSBURG

WARSCHAU
(WARSZAWA)

Geography and Planography, Plate 37

PLAN VON BERLIN.

Geography and Planography, Plate 38

Preussische Ruthen

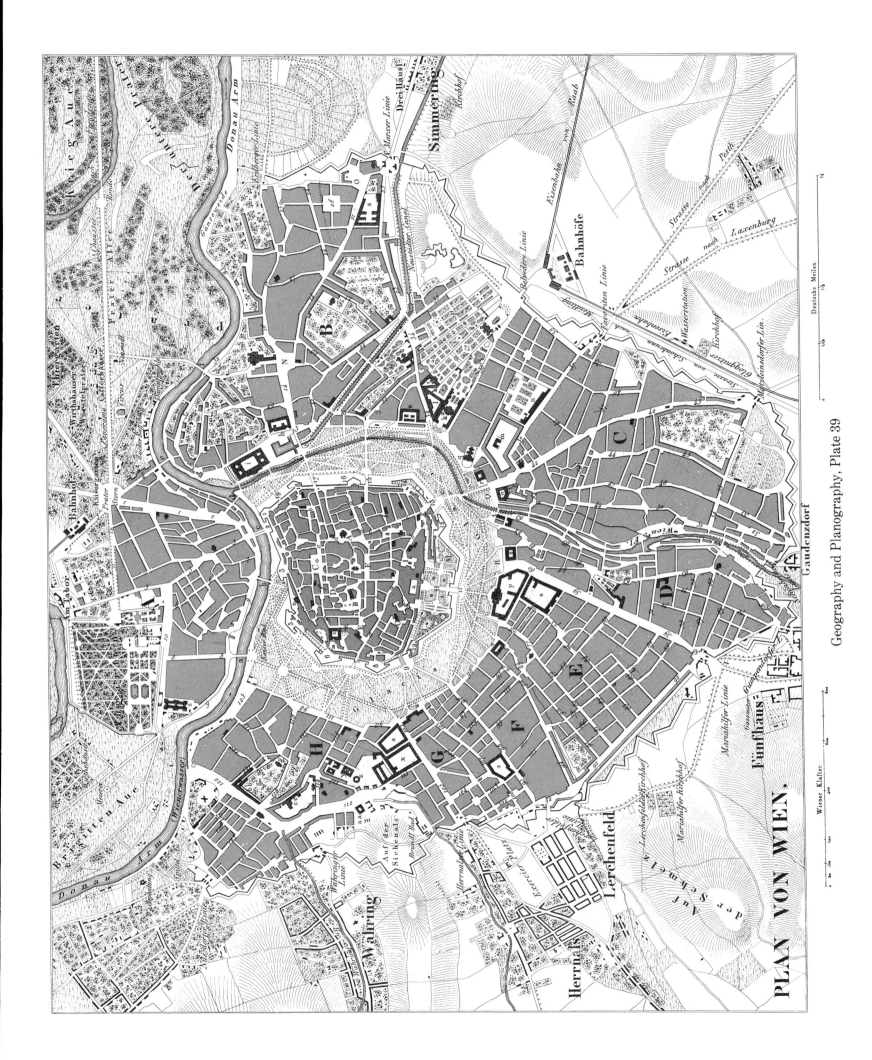

PLAN VON WIEN.

Geography and Planography, Plate 39

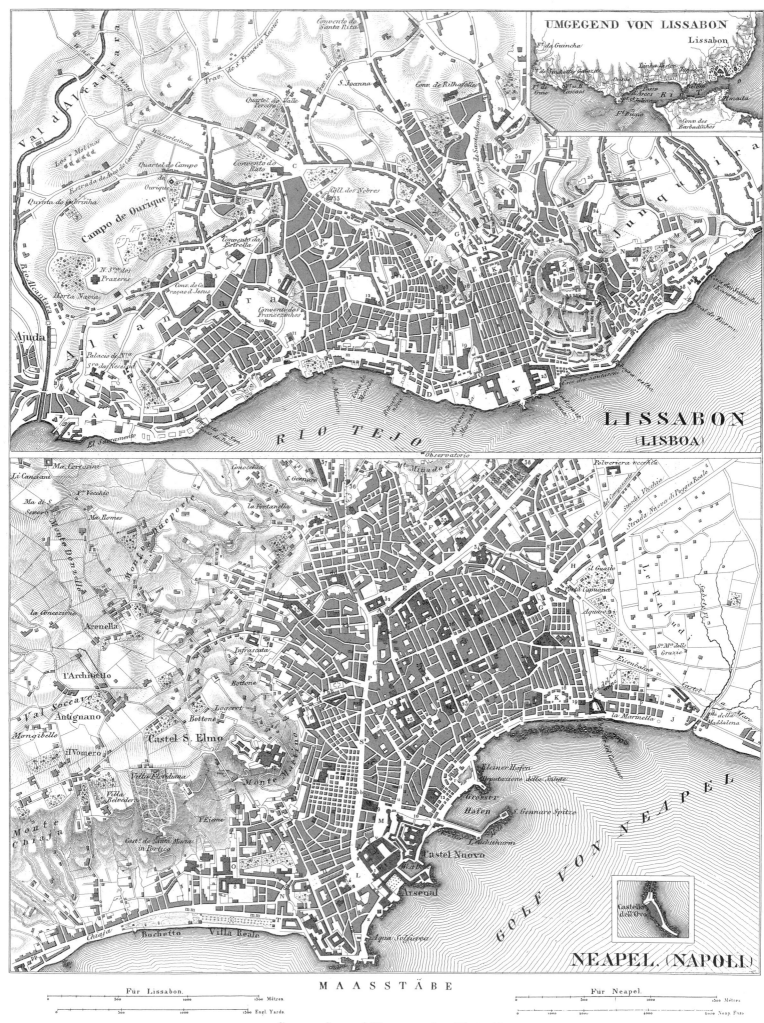

UMGEGEND VON LISSABON

Lissabon

LISSABON
(LISBOA)

NEAPEL. (NAPOLI)

Castello dell'Ovo

MAASSTÄBE

Für Lissabon.

Für Neapel.

Geography and Planography, Plate 40

40

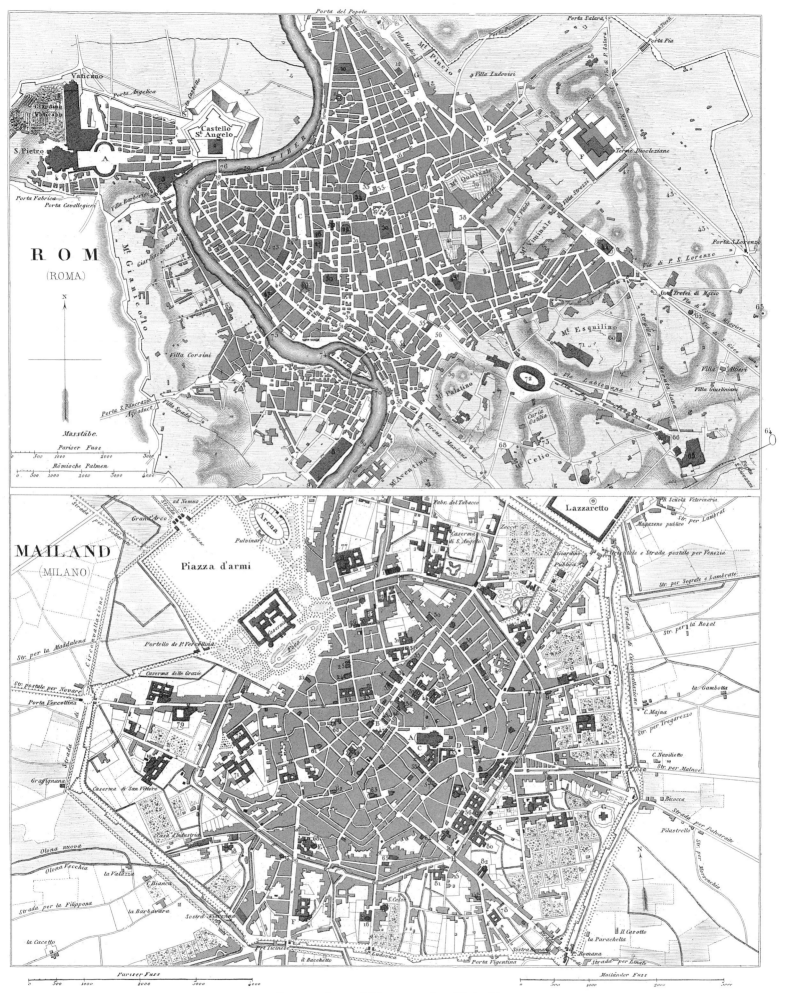

Geography and Planography, Plate 41

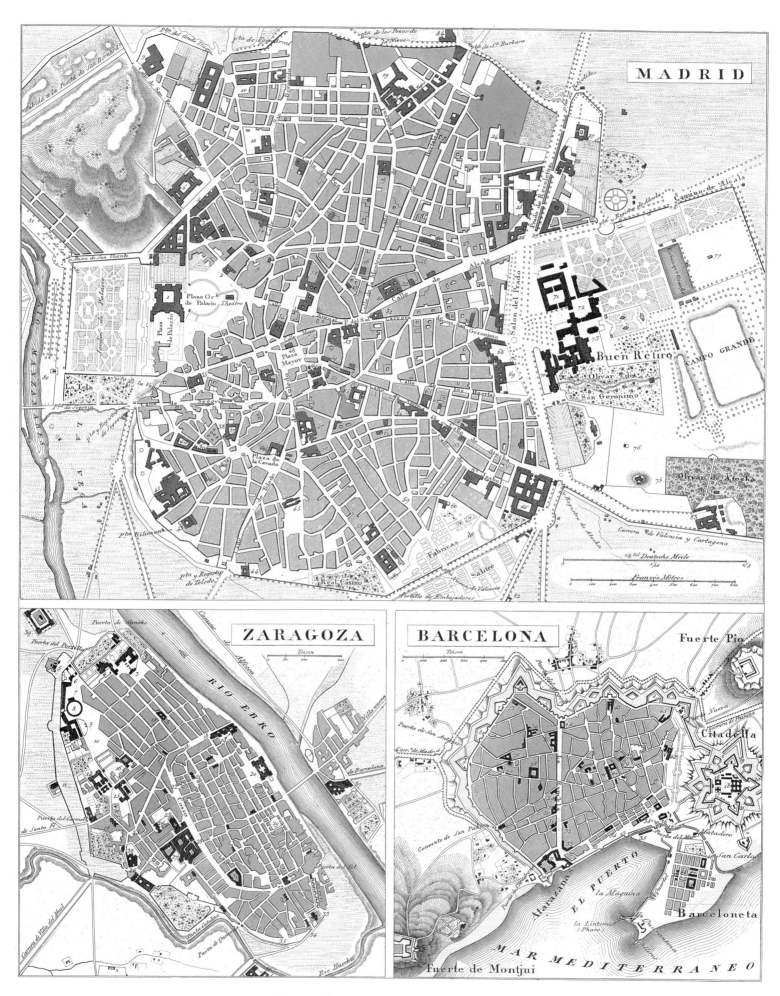

Geography and Planography, Plate 42

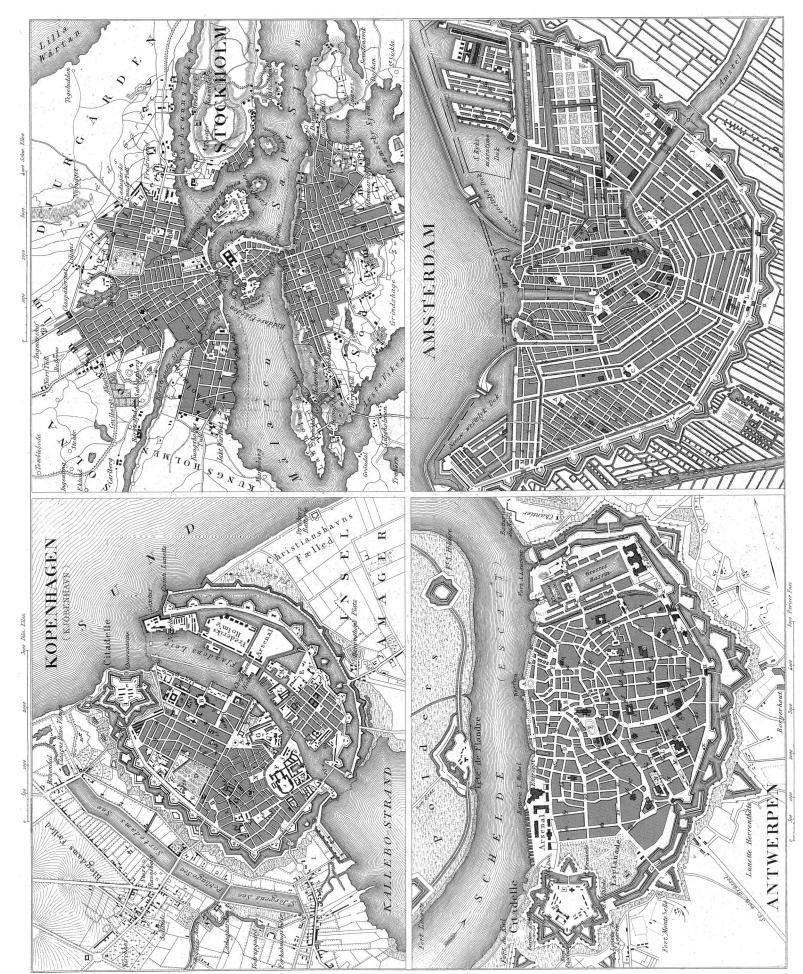

STOCKHOLM

AMSTERDAM

KOPENHAGEN (KIØBENHAVN)

ANTWERPEN

Geography and Planography, Plate 43

43

FLORENZ

MODENA

LIVORNO

ANCONA

Geography and Planography, Plate 44

44

History, Plate 1

45

History, Plate 2

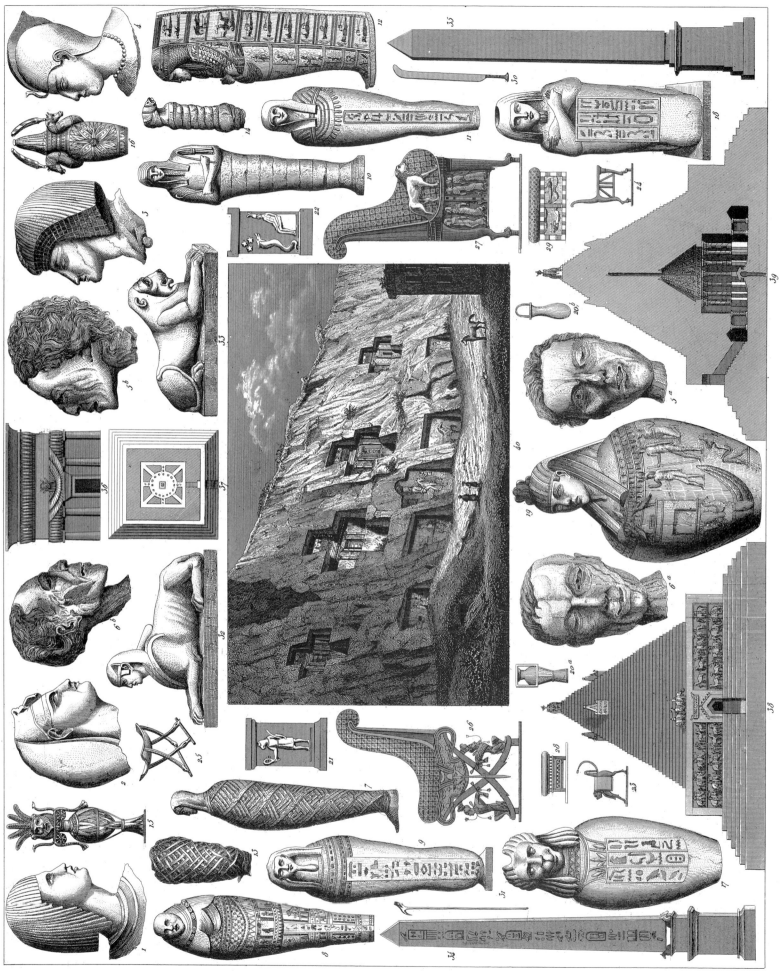

History, Plate 3

47

History, Plate 4

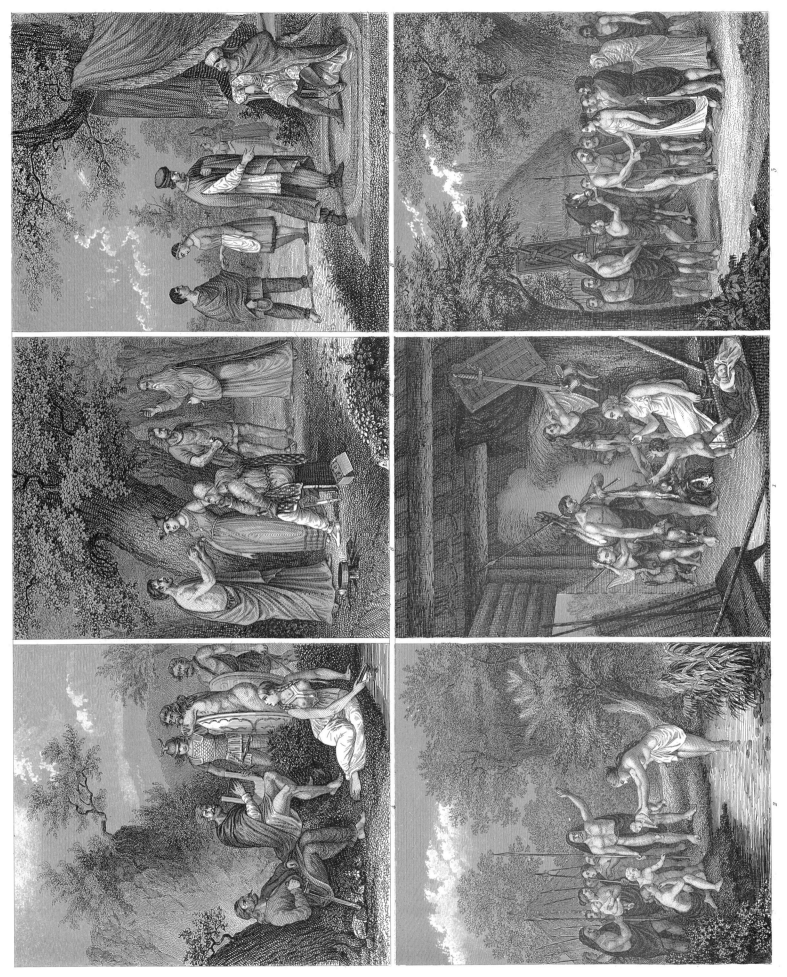

History, Plate 5

History, Plate 7

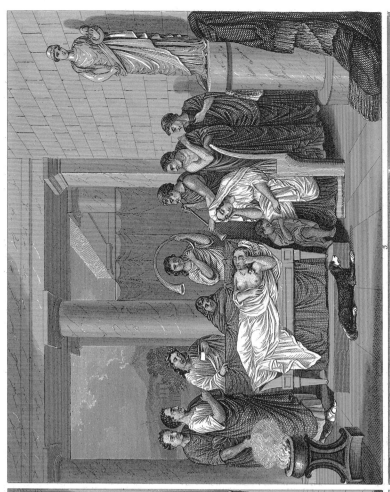

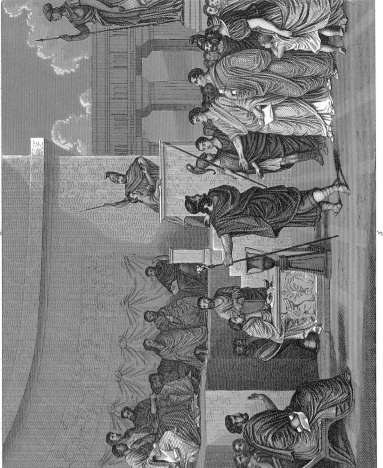

History, Plate 8

History, Plate 9

53

Maasstäbe in Metres.

History, Plate 12

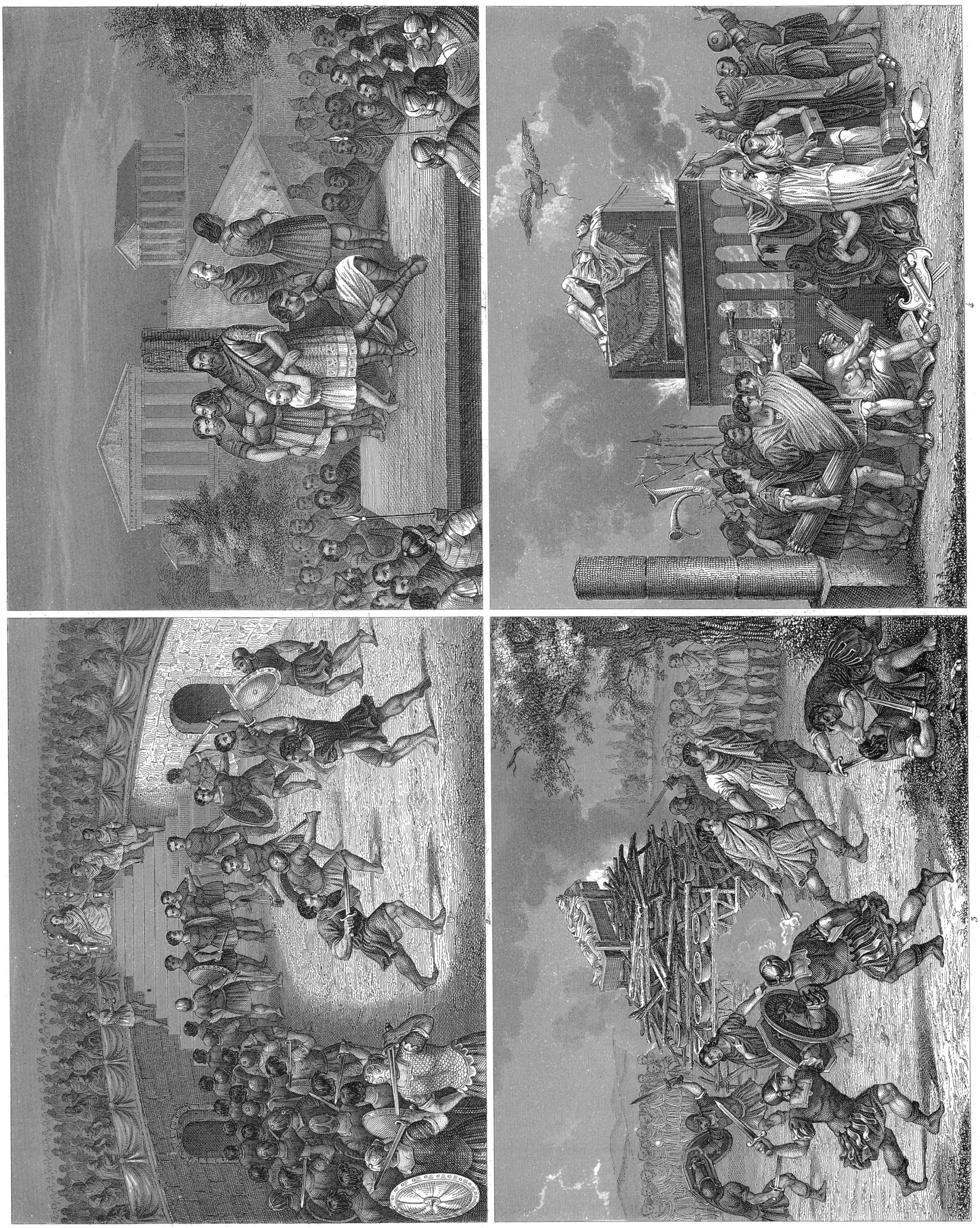

History, Plate 13

History, Plate 14

58

Fig. 2

Figur 1.

History, Plate 16

61

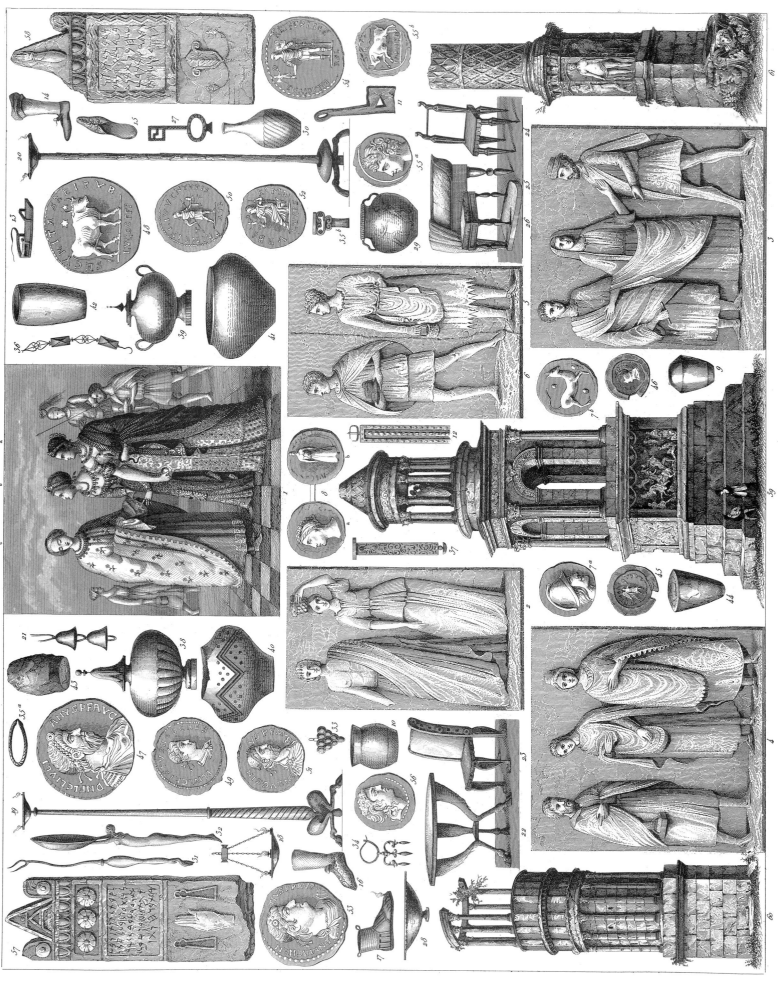

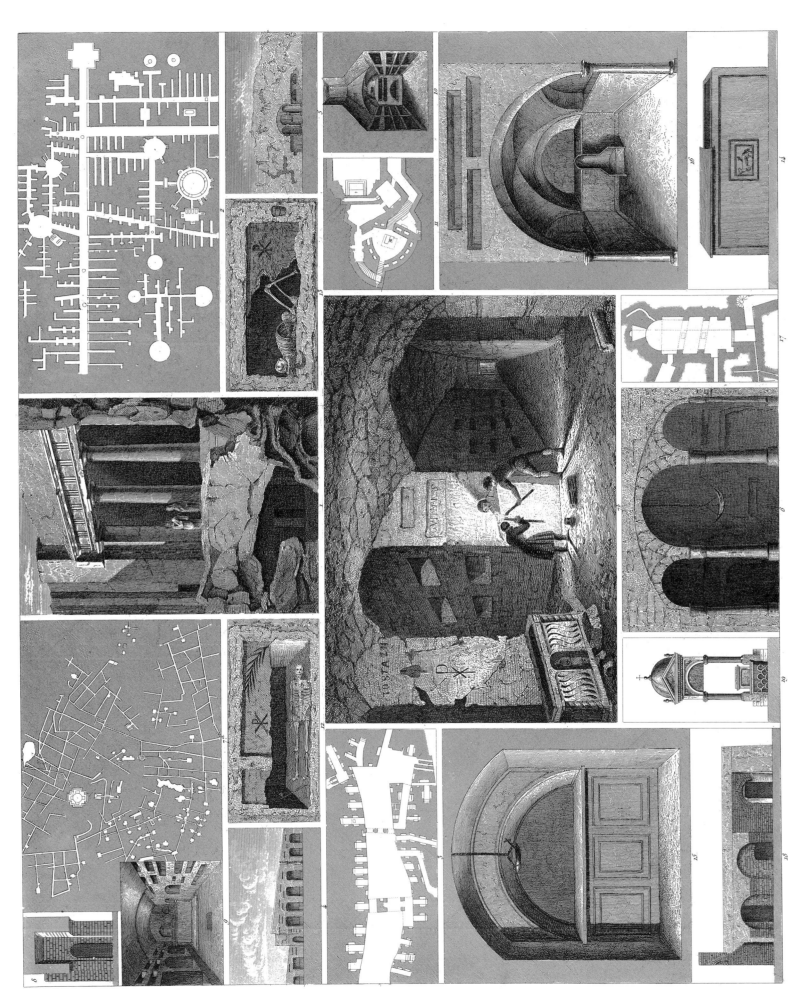

History, Plate 20

History, Plate 21

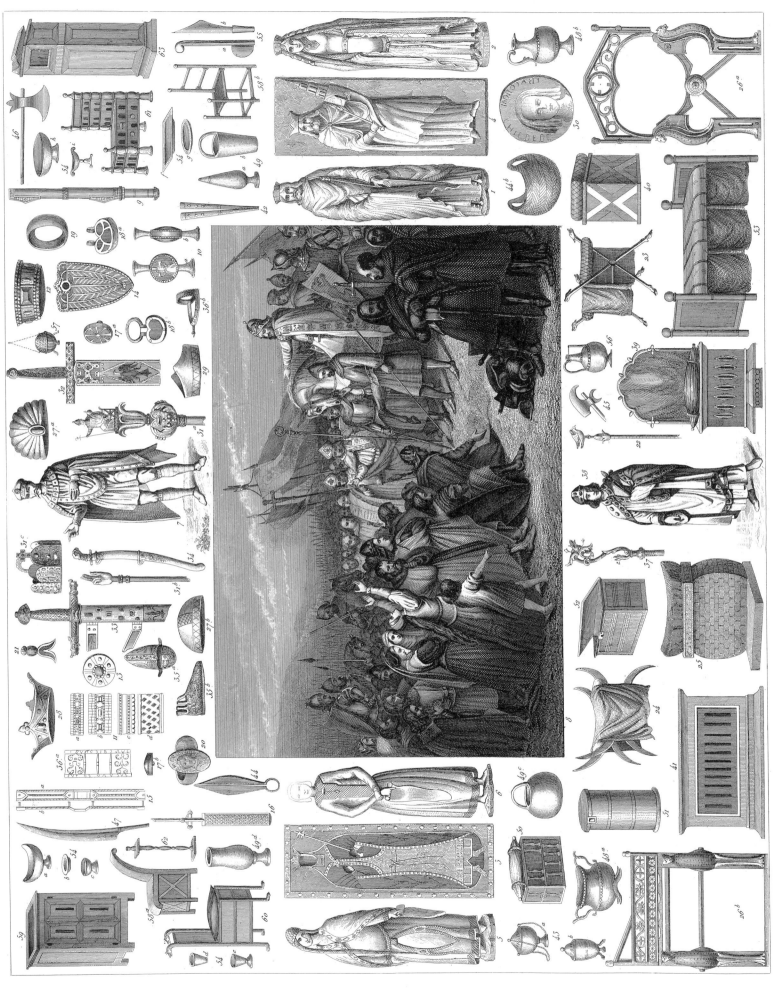

History, Plate 22

66

History, Plate 23

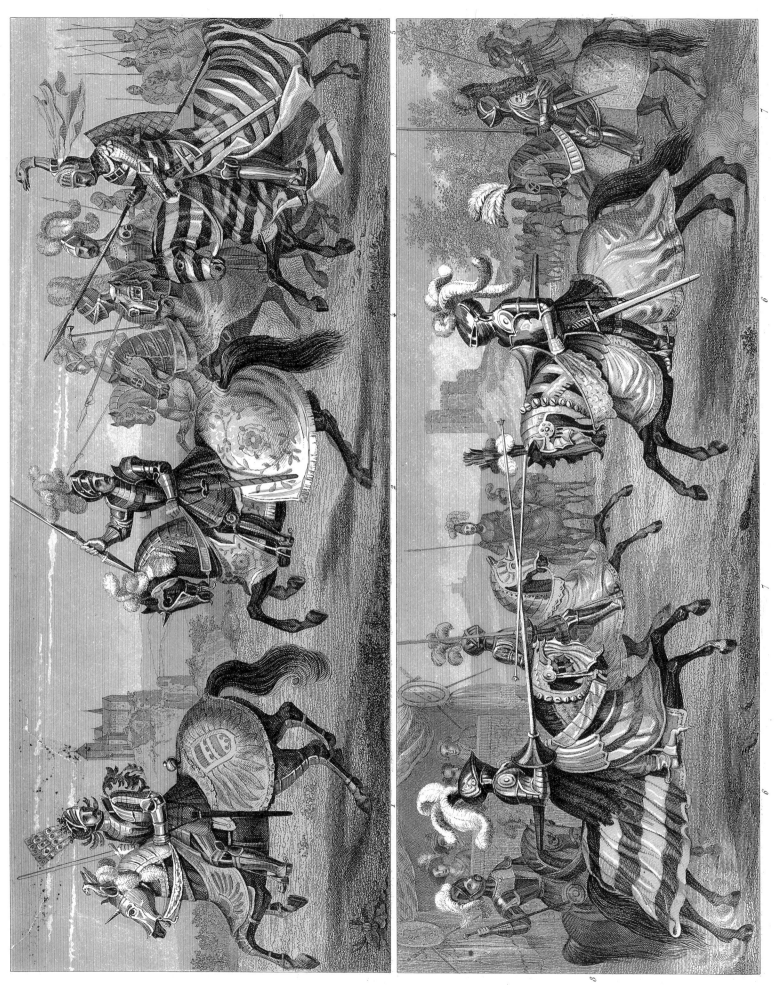

History, Plate 24

History, Plate 25

History, Plate 26

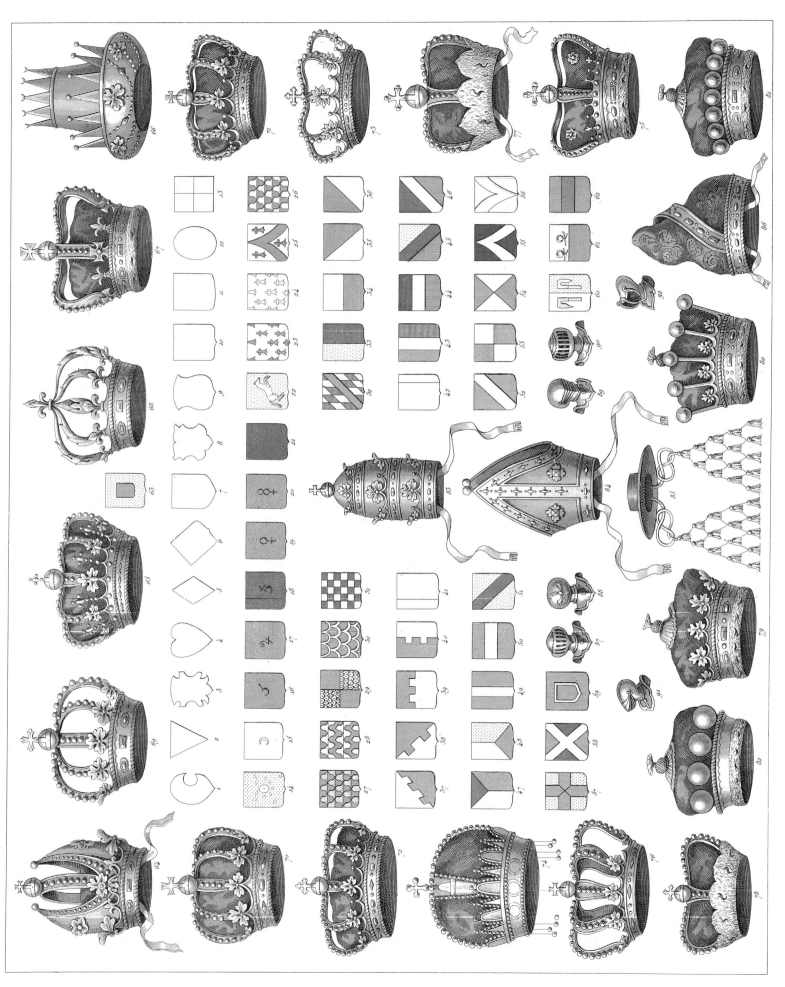

History, Plate 30

History, Plate 31

History, Plate 32

History, Plate 33

History, Plate 34

History, Plate 36

History, Plate 37

History, Plate 38

History, Plate 39 was the last History plate.

Ethnology, Plate 1

Ethnology, Plate 2

Ethnology, Plate 3

Ethnology, Plate 4

Ethnology, Plate 5

Ethnology, Plate 6

Ethnology, Plate 7

Ethnology, Plate 8

Ethnology, Plate 9

Ethnology, Plate 10

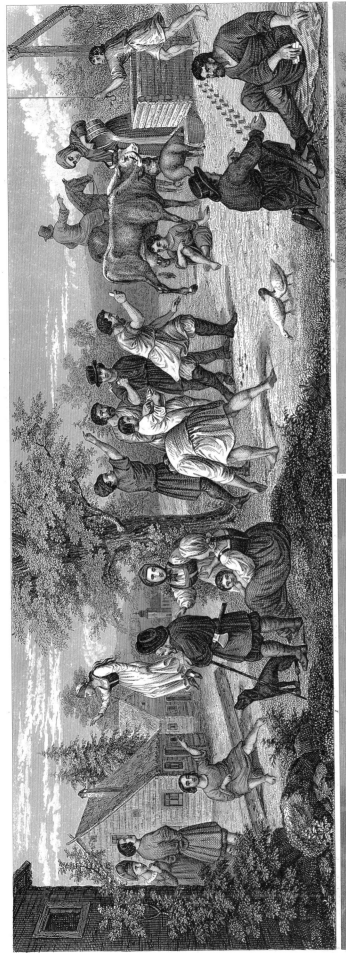

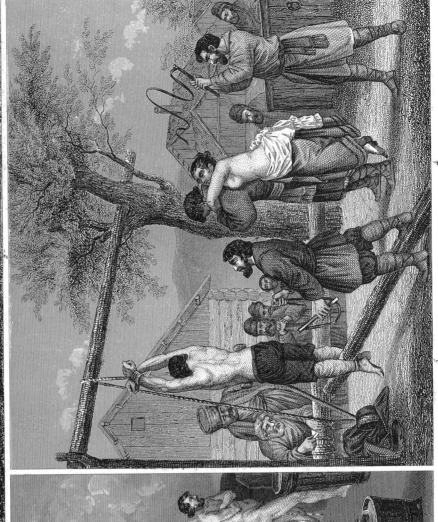

Ethnology, Plate 11

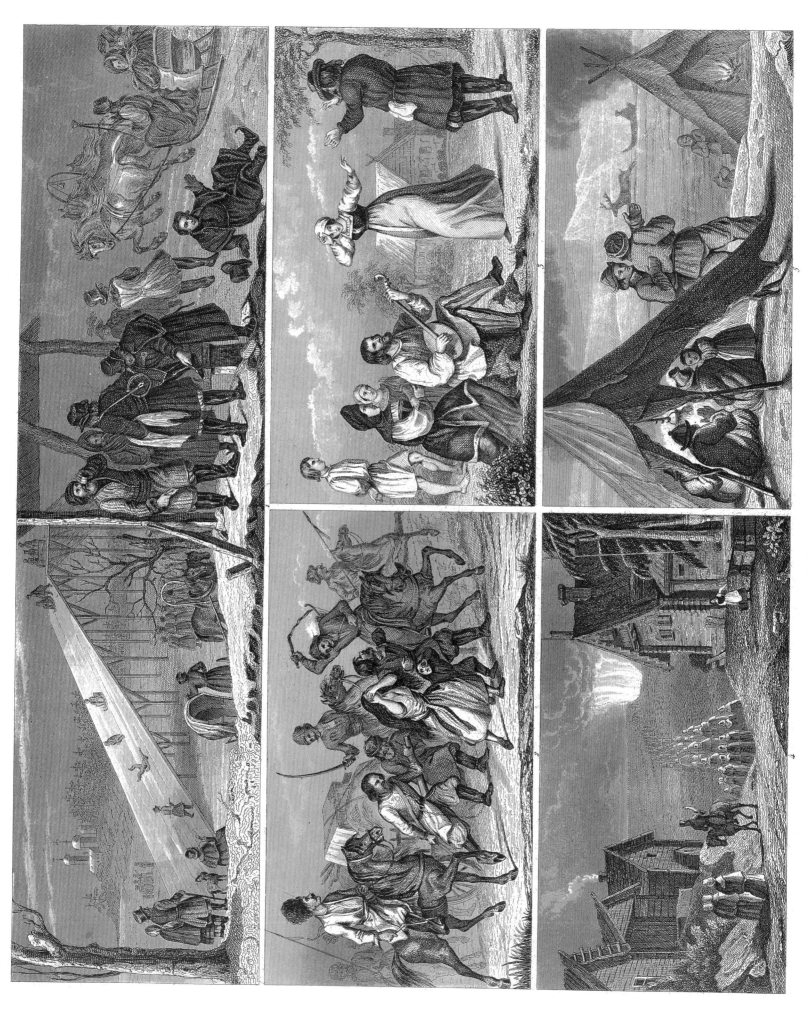

Ethnology, Plate 12

Ethnology, Plate 13

Ethnology, Plate 14

Ethnology, Plate 15

Ethnology, Plate 16

Ethnology, Plate 17

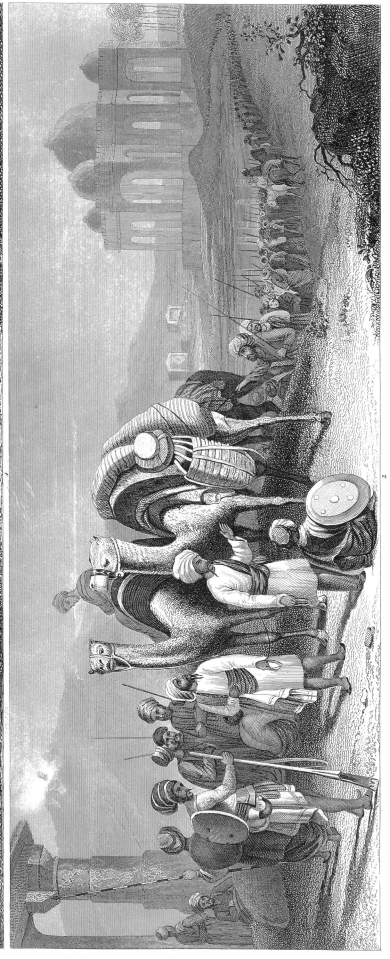

Ethnology, Plate 19

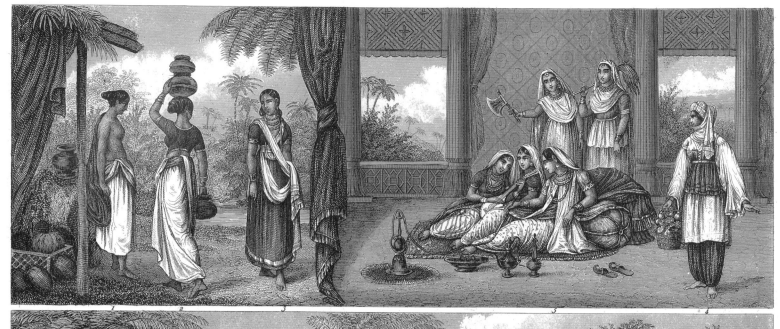

Ethnology, Plate 20

Ethnology, Plate 21

Ethnology, Plate 22

Ethnology, Plate 23

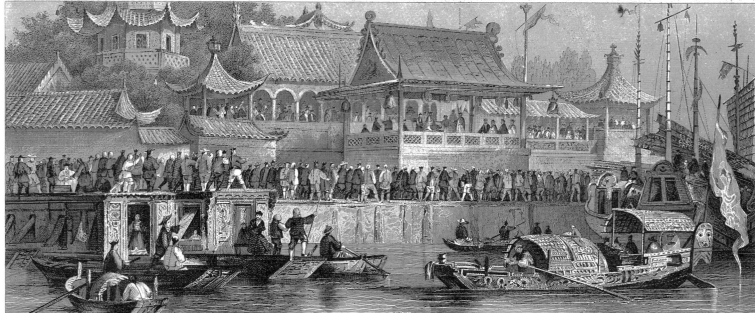

Ethnology, Plate 24

Ethnology, Plate 25

Ethnology, Plate 26

Ethnology, Plate 27

Ethnology, Plate 28

Ethnology, Plate 29

Ethnology, Plate 30

Ethnology, Plate 31

Ethnology, Plate 32

Ethnology, Plate 33

Ethnology, Plate 34

Ethnology, Plate 35

Ethnology, Plate 36

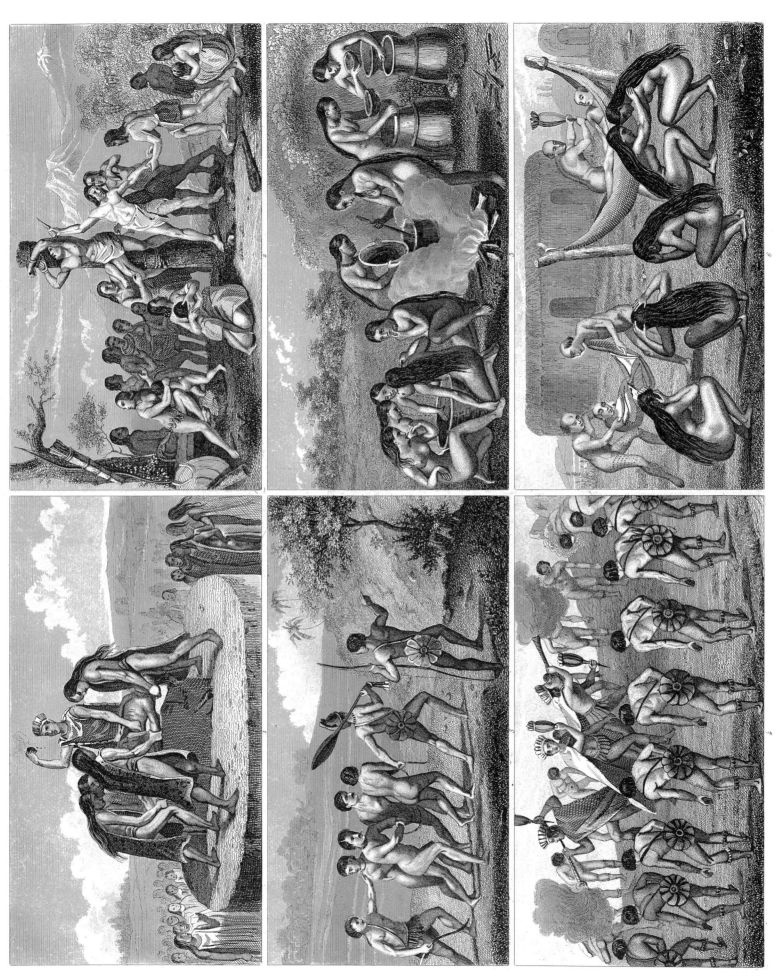

Ethnology, Plate 38

Ethnology, Plate 39

123

Ethnology, Plate 40

Ethnology, Plate 41

Ethnology, Plate 42

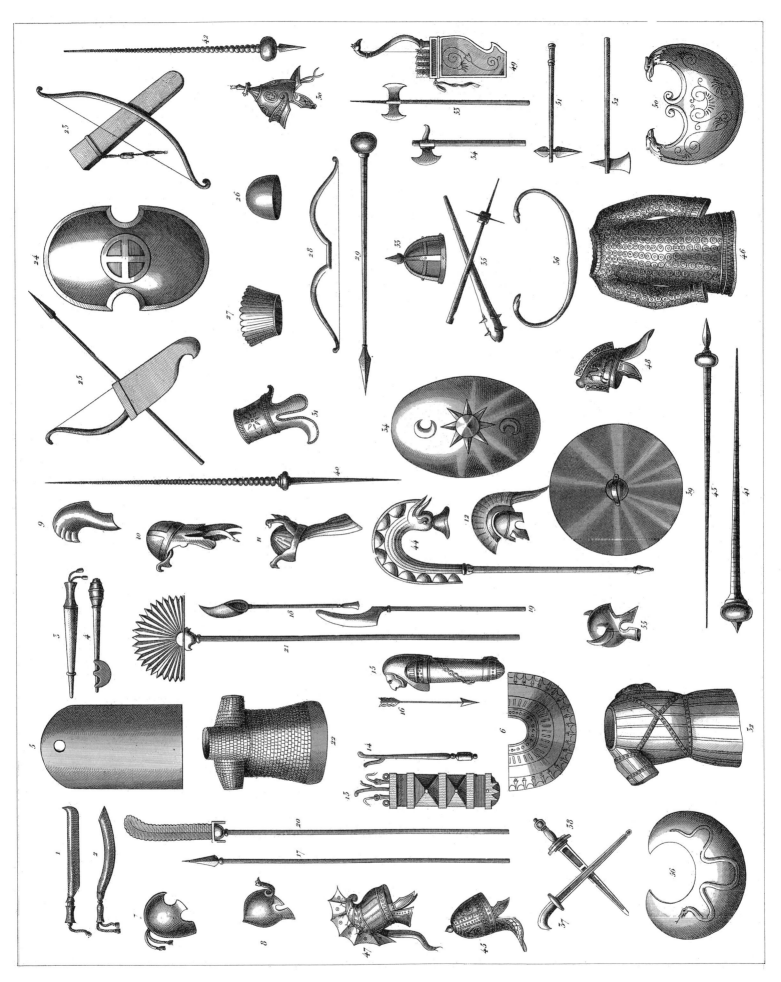

Military Sciences, Plate 1

127

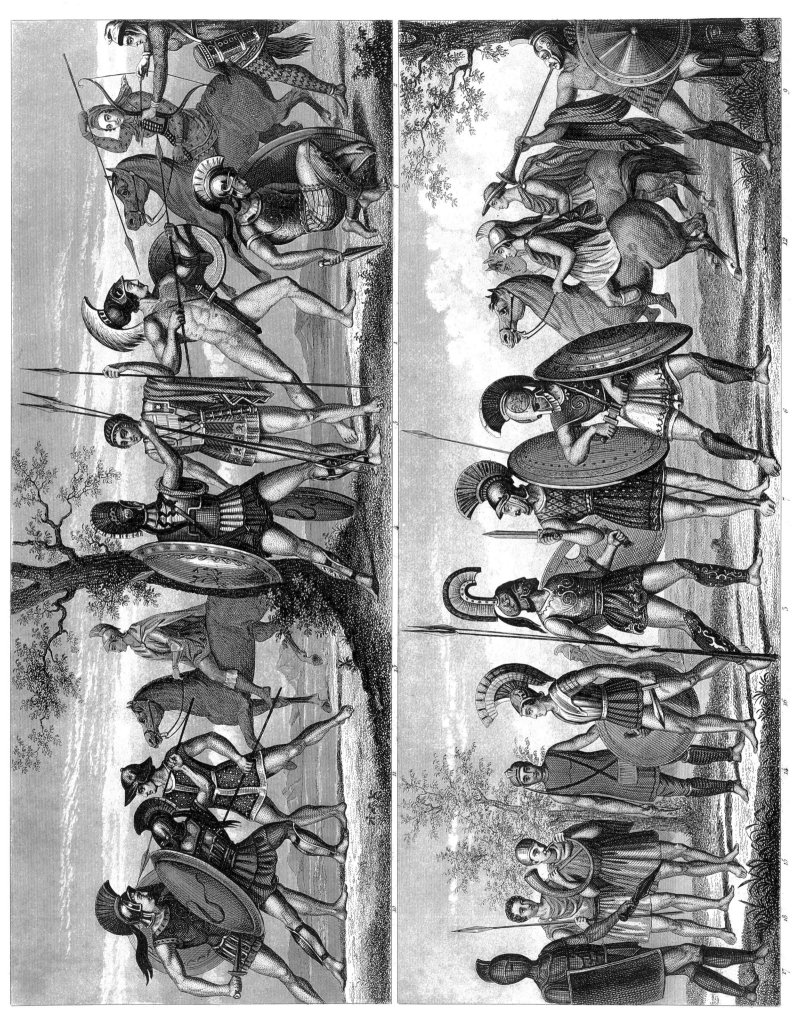

Military Sciences, Plate 2

128

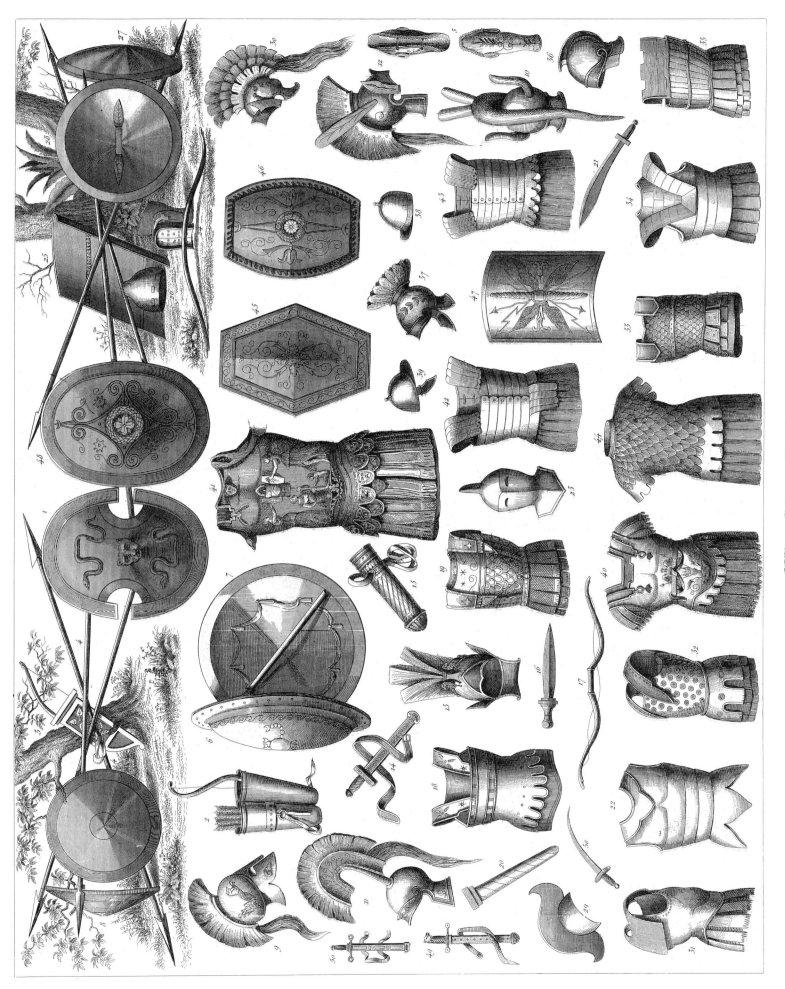

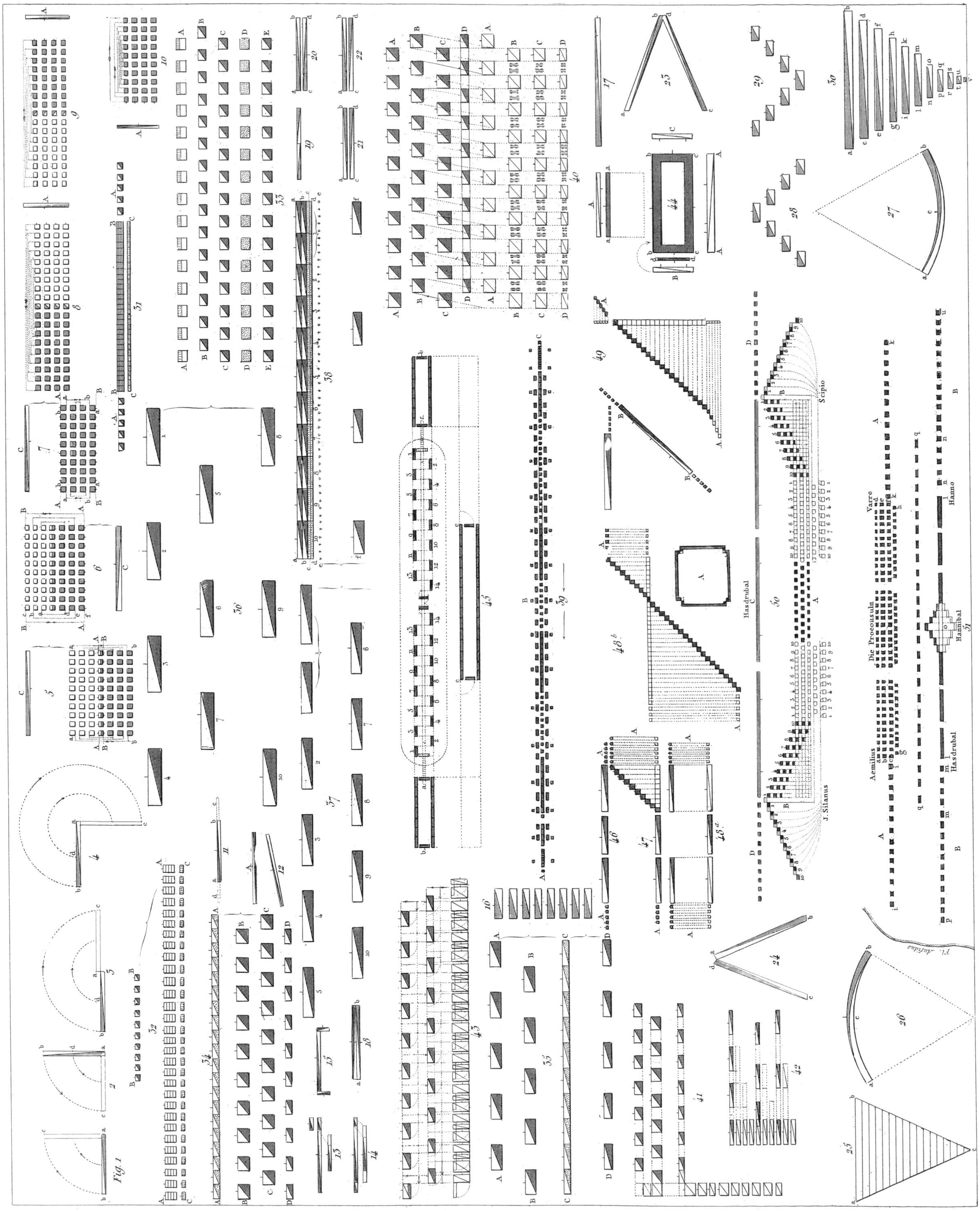

Military Sciences, Plate 4

Military Sciences, Plate 6

132

133

Military Sciences, Plate 8

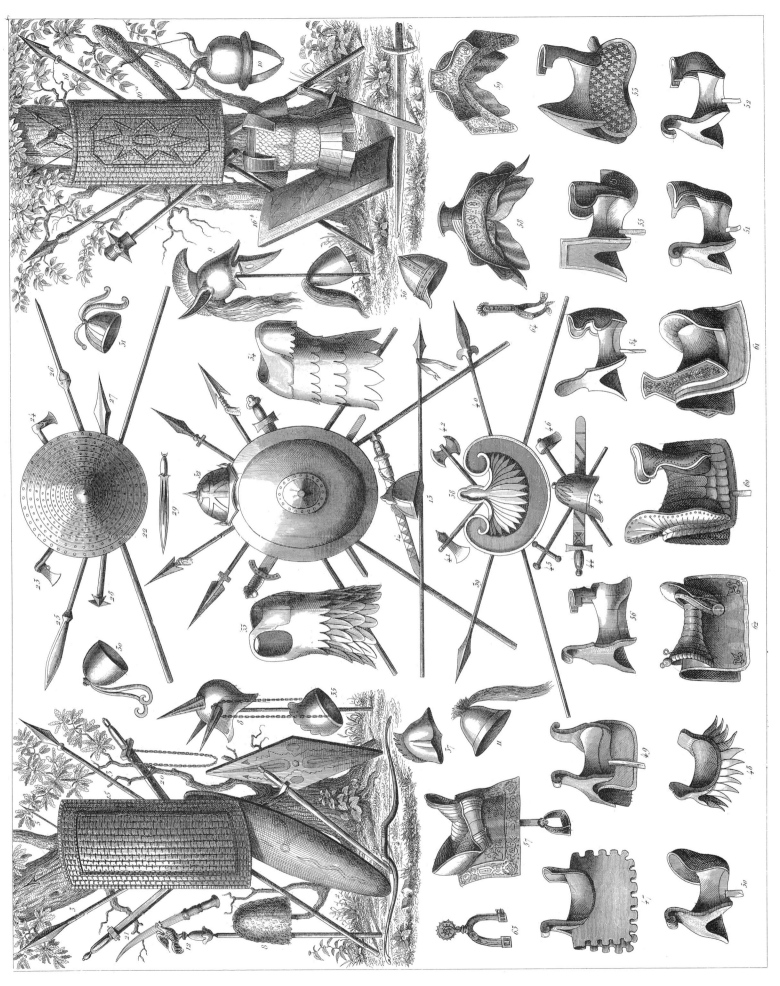

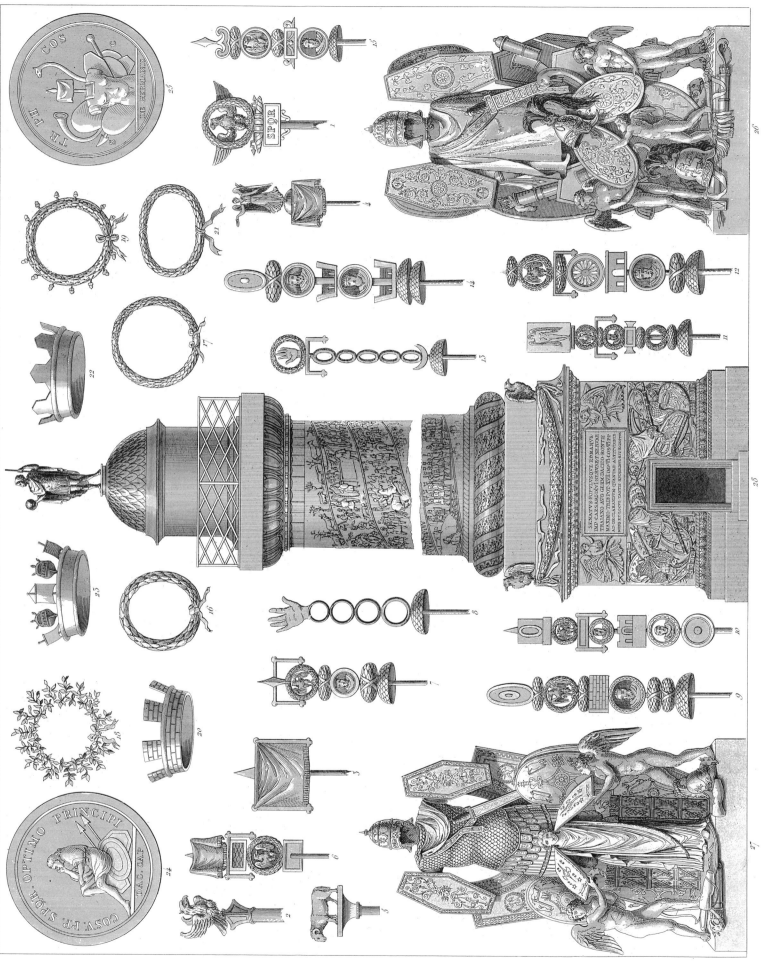

Military Sciences, Plate 10

Military Sciences, Plate 11

Military Sciences, Plate 13

139

Military Sciences, Plate 14

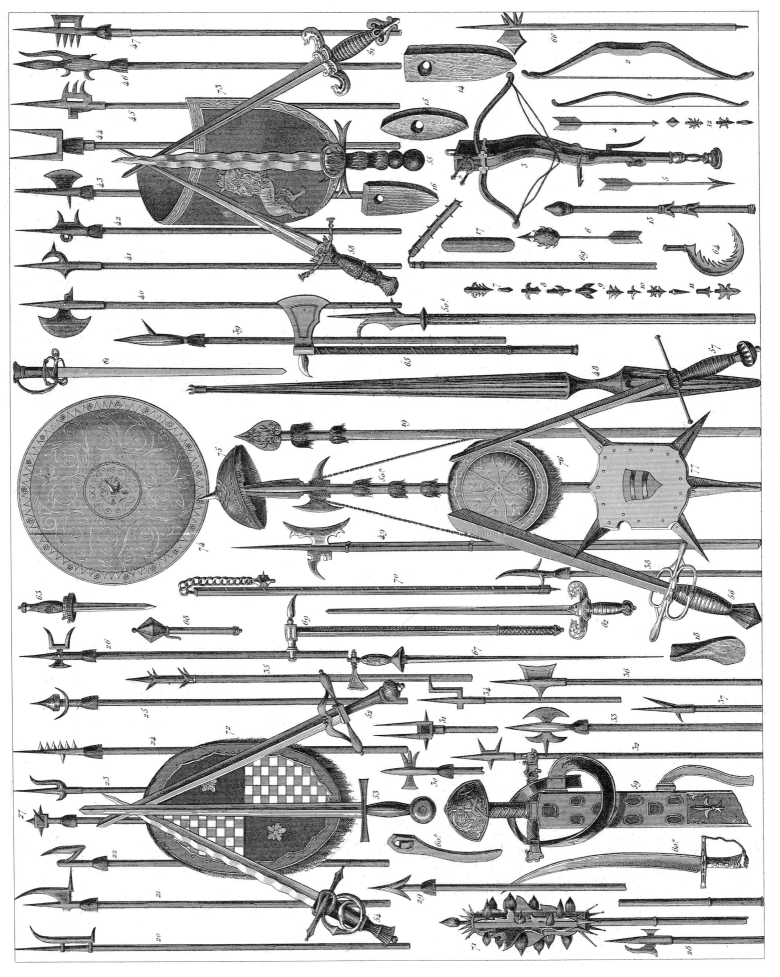

Military Sciences, Plate 15

141

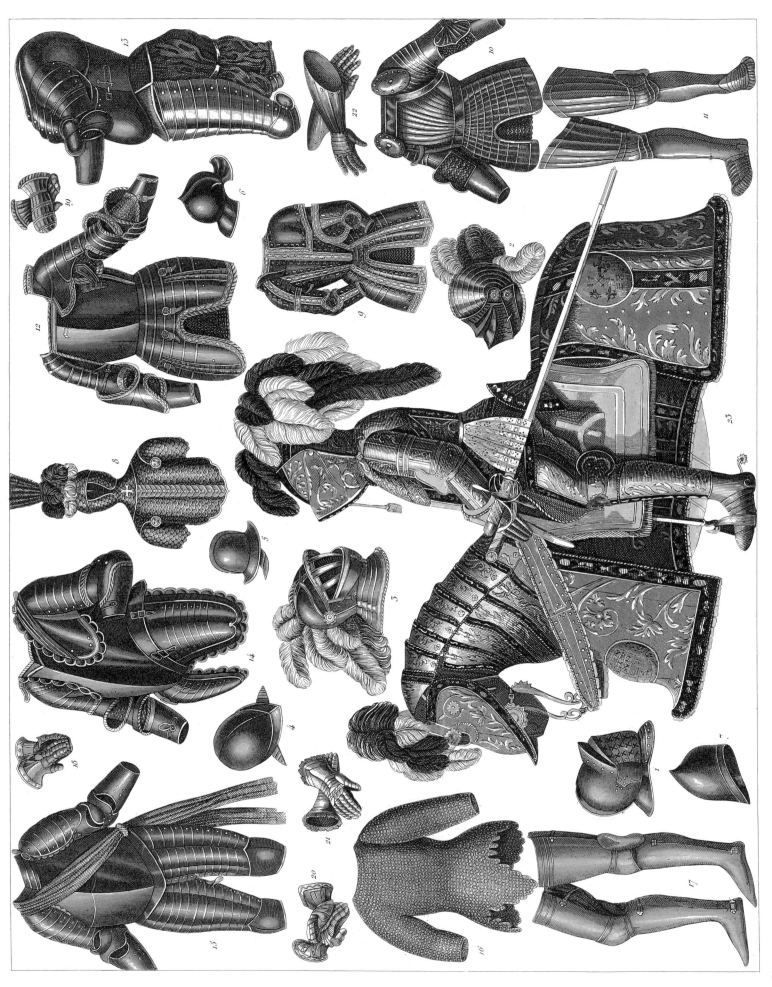

Military Sciences, Plate 16

Military Sciences, Plate 17

Military Sciences, Plate 18

Military Sciences, Plate 19

Military Sciences, Plate 20

Military Sciences, Plate 21

Military Sciences, Plate 22

148

Military Sciences, Plate 23

149

Military Sciences, Plate 24

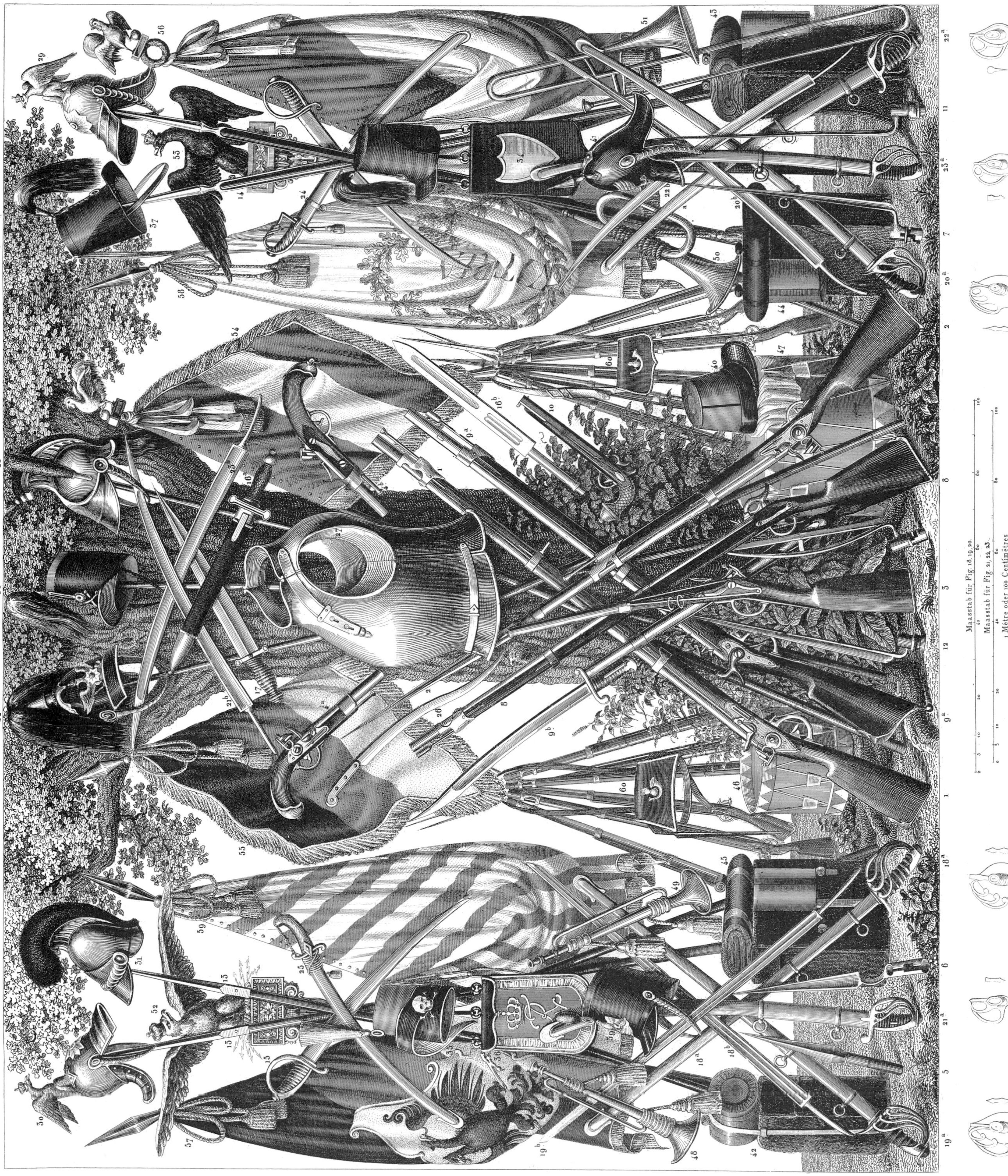

Military Sciences, Plate 25

Military Sciences, Plate 26

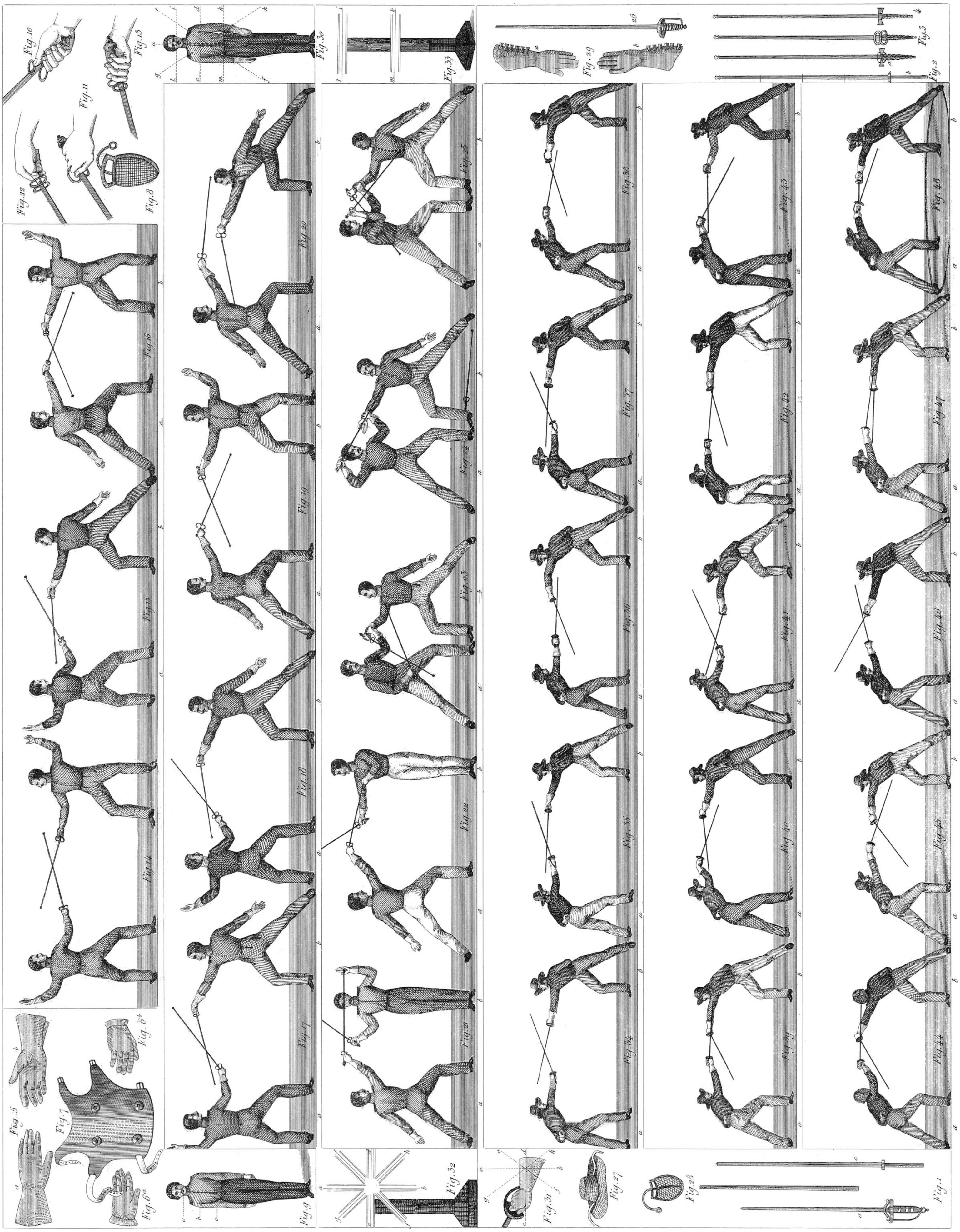

Military Sciences, Plate 27

153

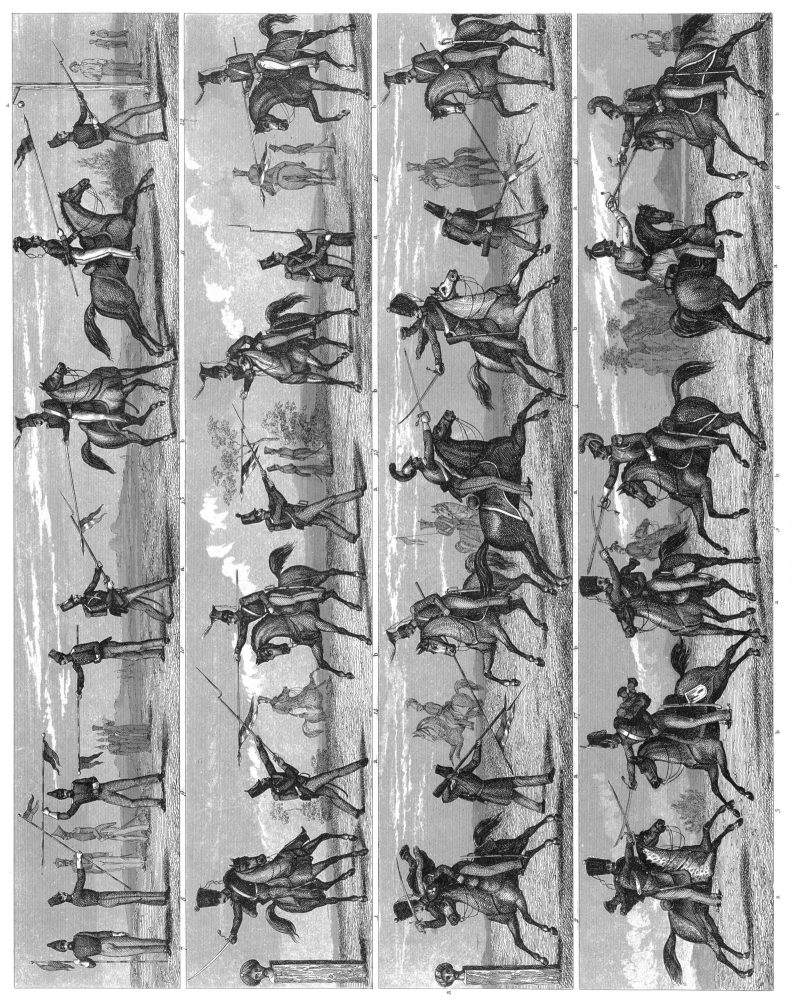

Military Sciences, Plate 28

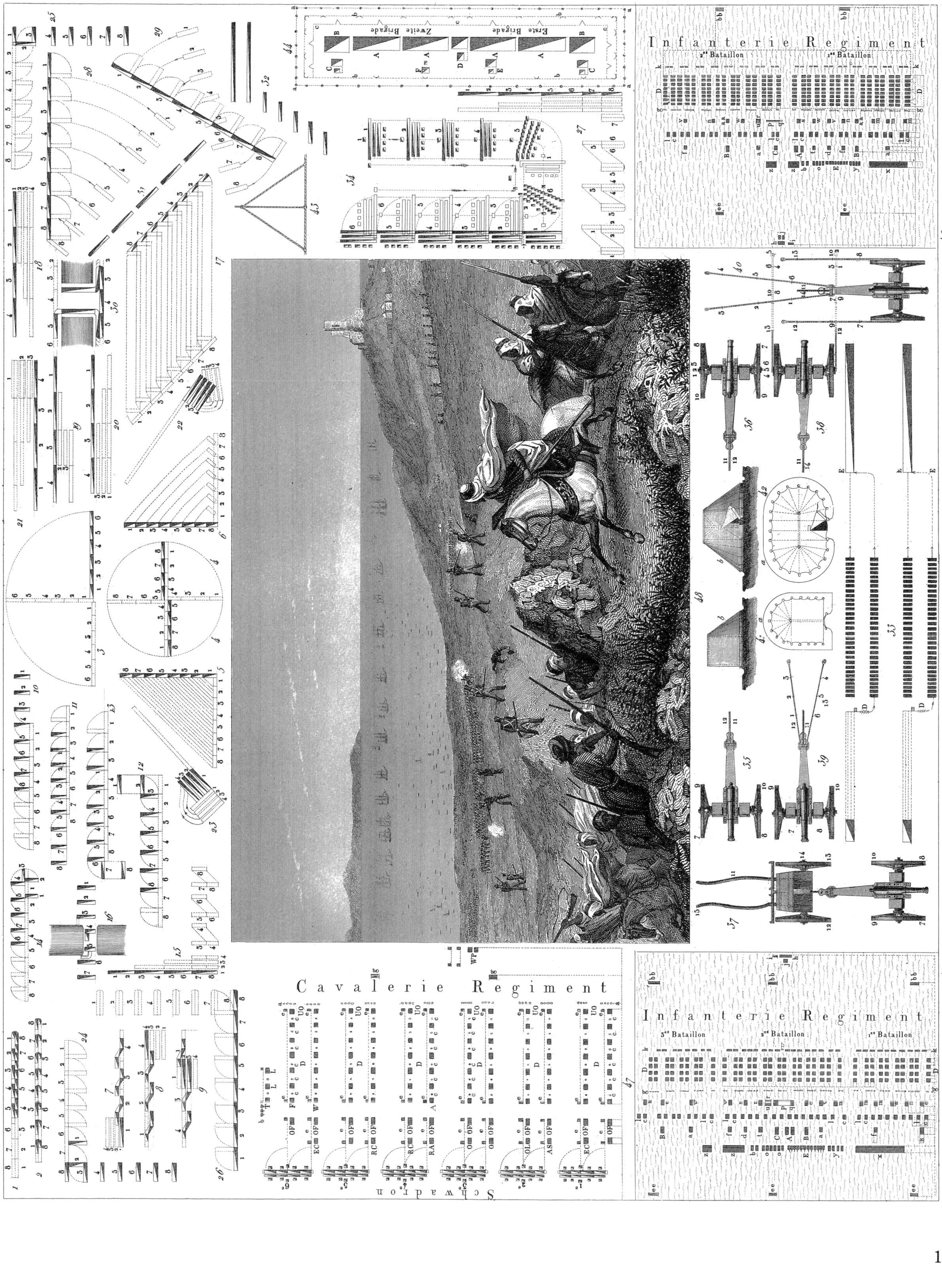

Zweite Brigade

Erste Brigade

Infanterie Regiment

2tes Bataillon

1tes Bataillon

Cavalerie Regiment

Schwadron

Infanterie Regiment

3tes Bataillon

2tes Bataillon

1tes Bataillon

Military Sciences, Plate 30

Military Sciences, Plate 31

157

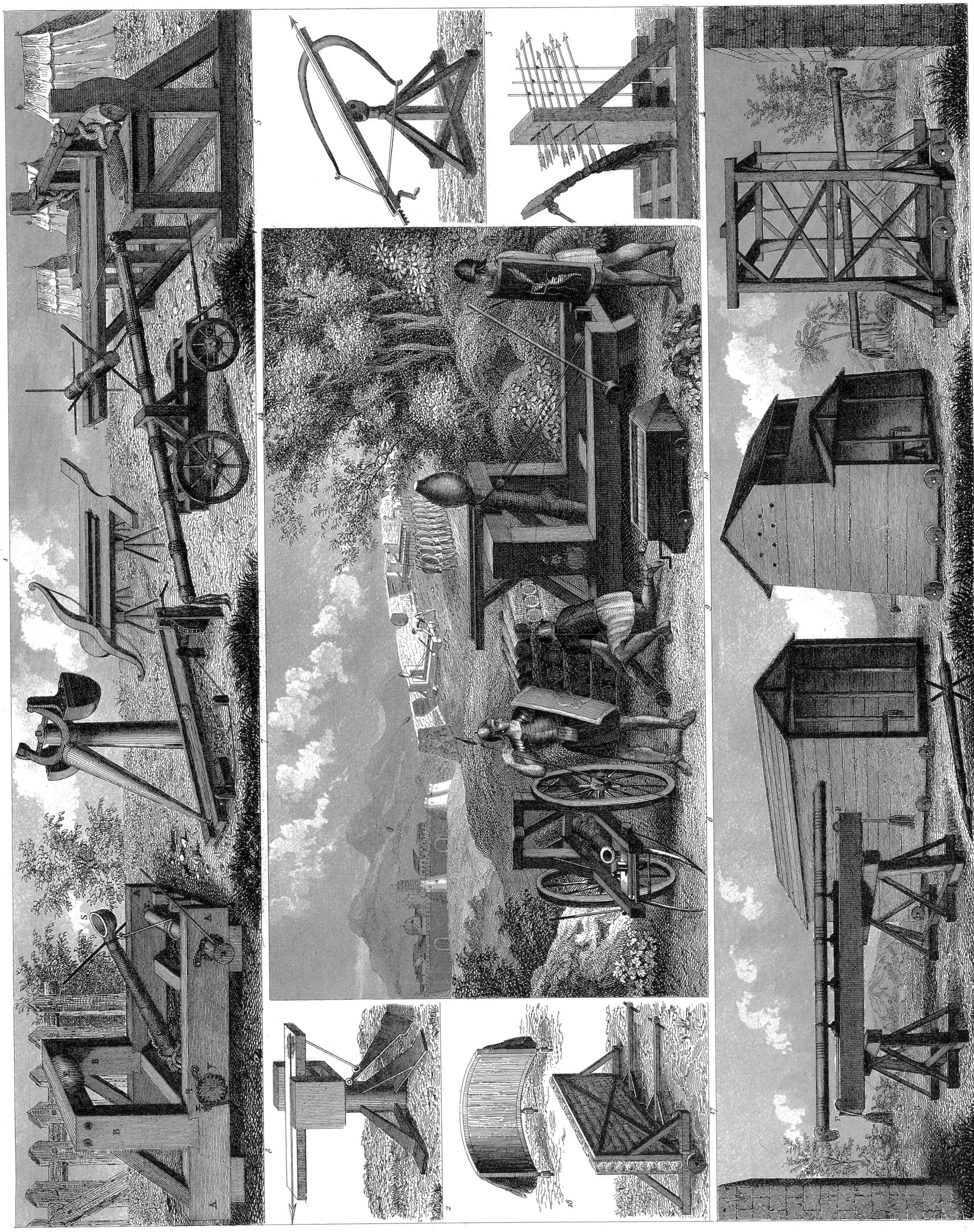

Military Sciences, Plate 33

Military Sciences, Plate 34

Military Sciences, Plate 35

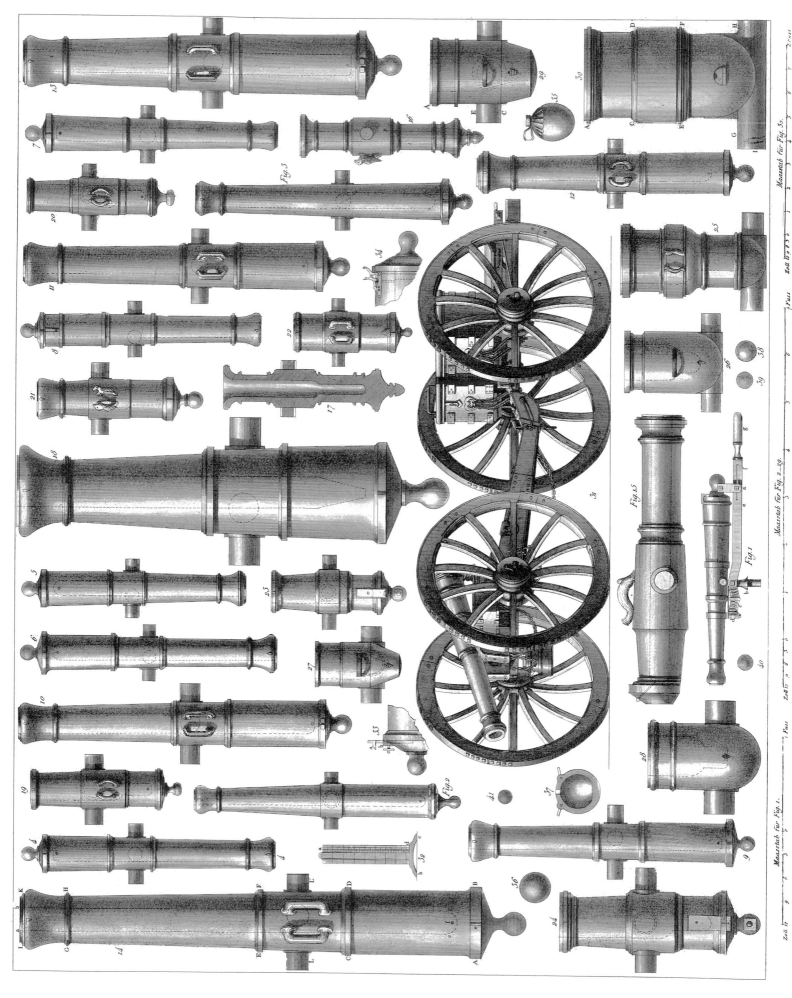

Military Sciences, Plate 36

162

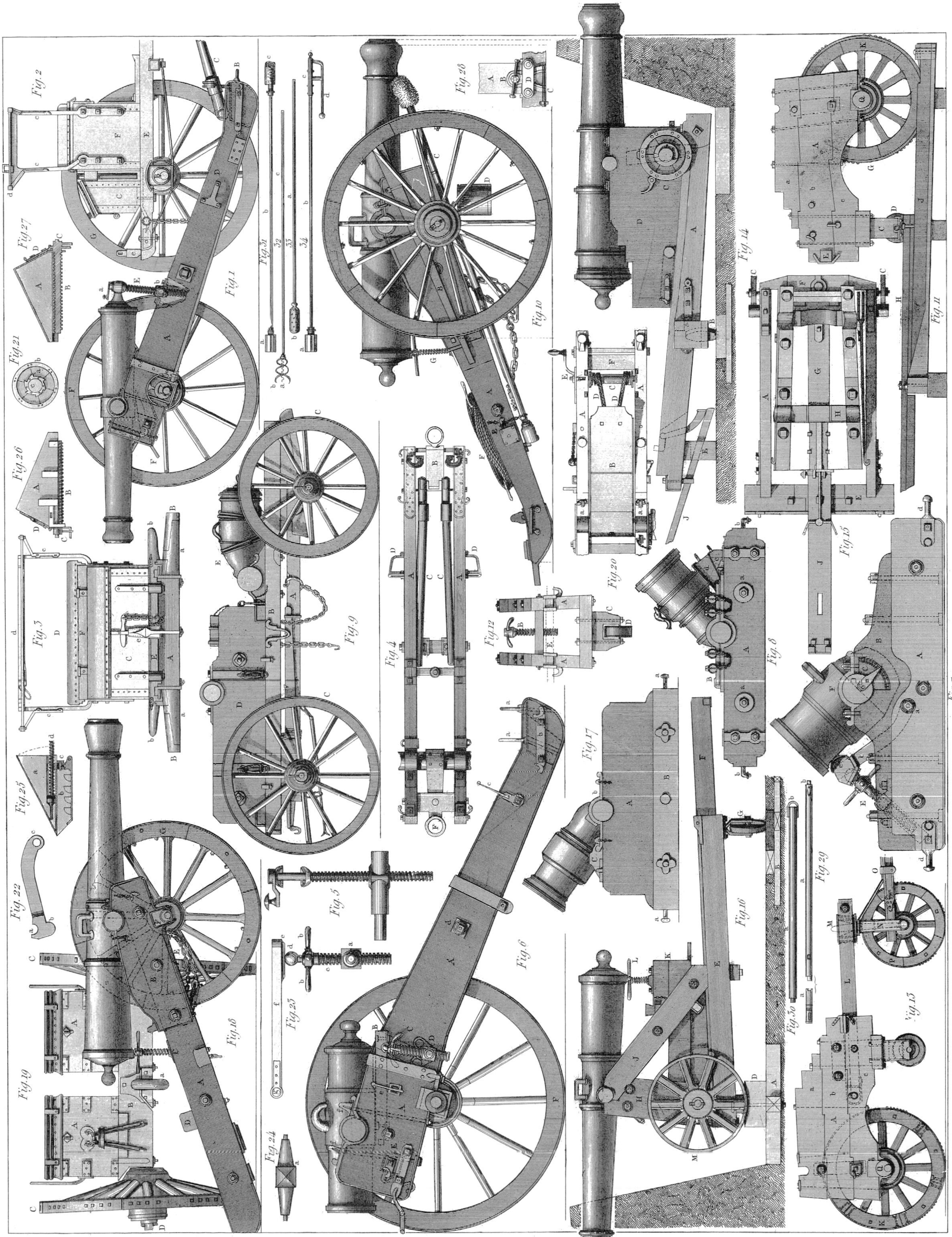

Military Sciences, Plate 37

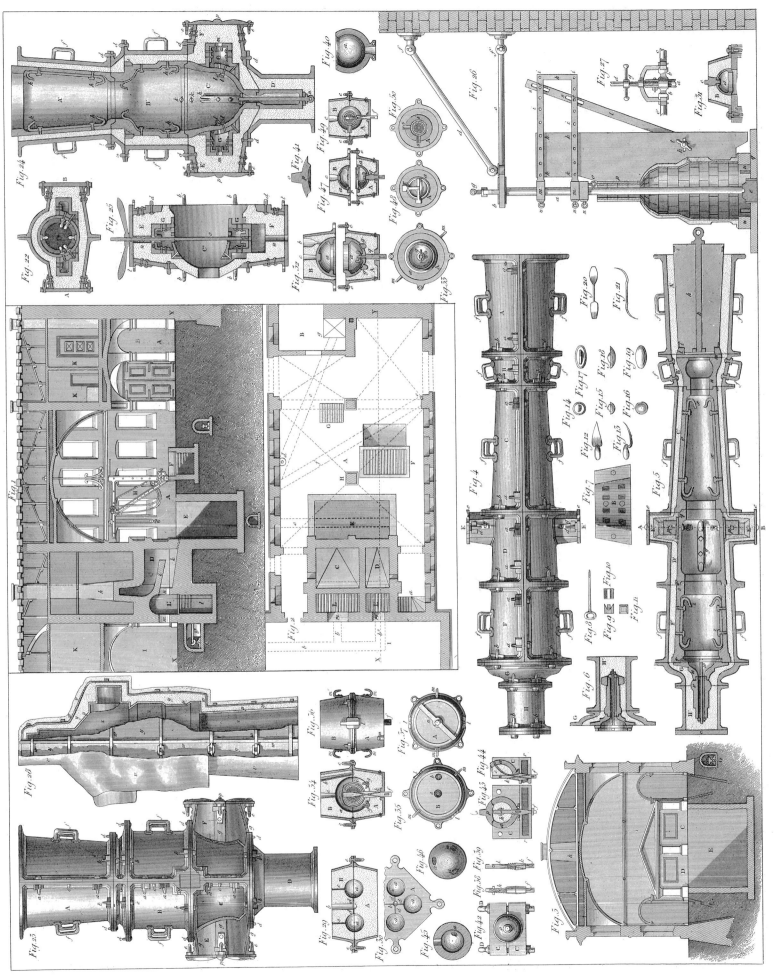

Military Sciences, Plate 39

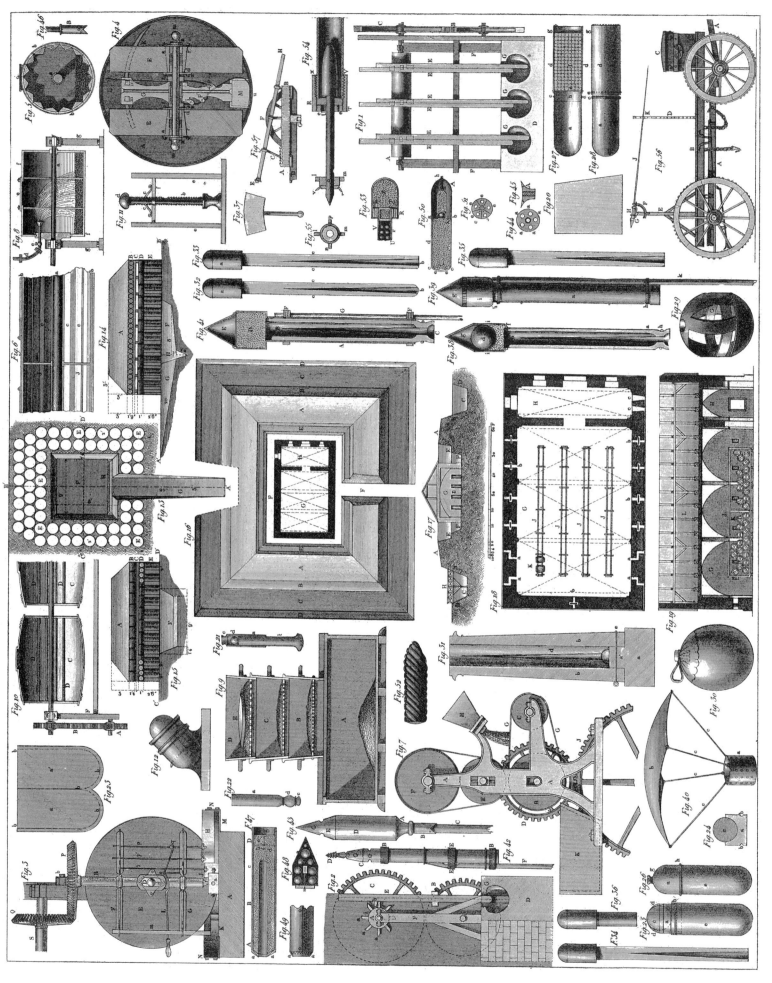

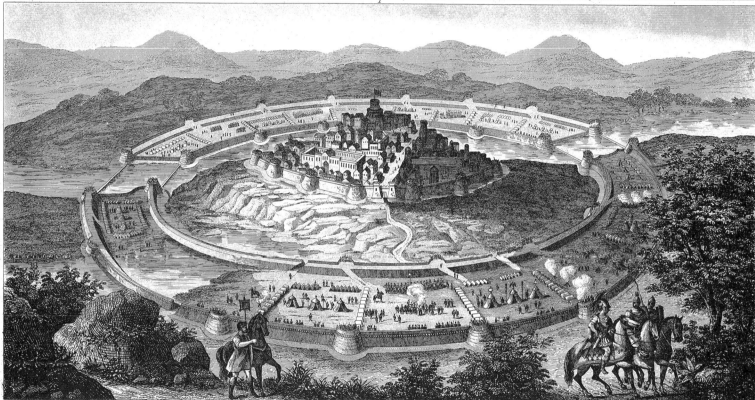

Military Sciences, Plate 41

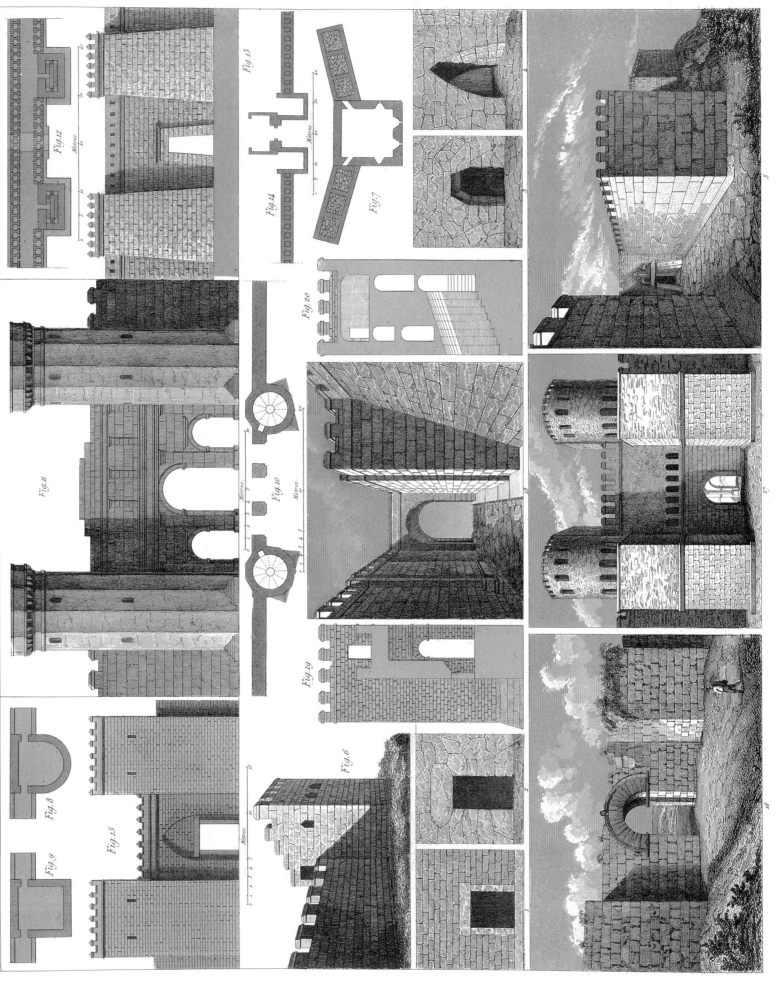

Military Sciences, Plate 42

Military Sciences, Plate 43

Military Sciences, Plate 44

170

Military Sciences, Plate 45

171

Military Sciences, Plate 46

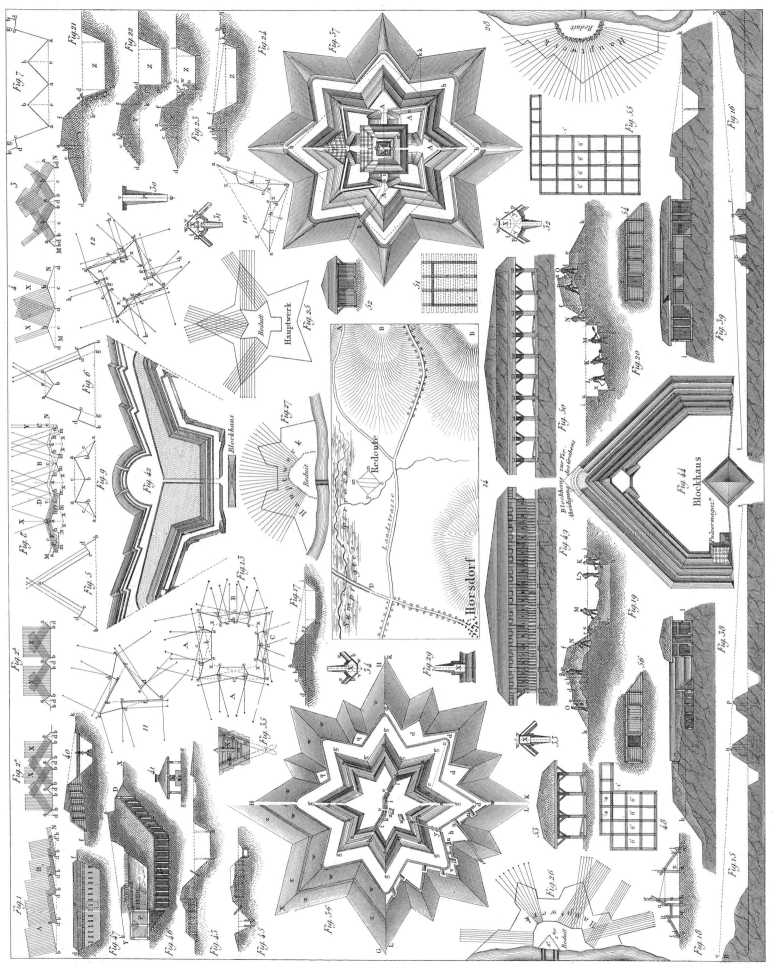

Military Sciences, Plate 47

173

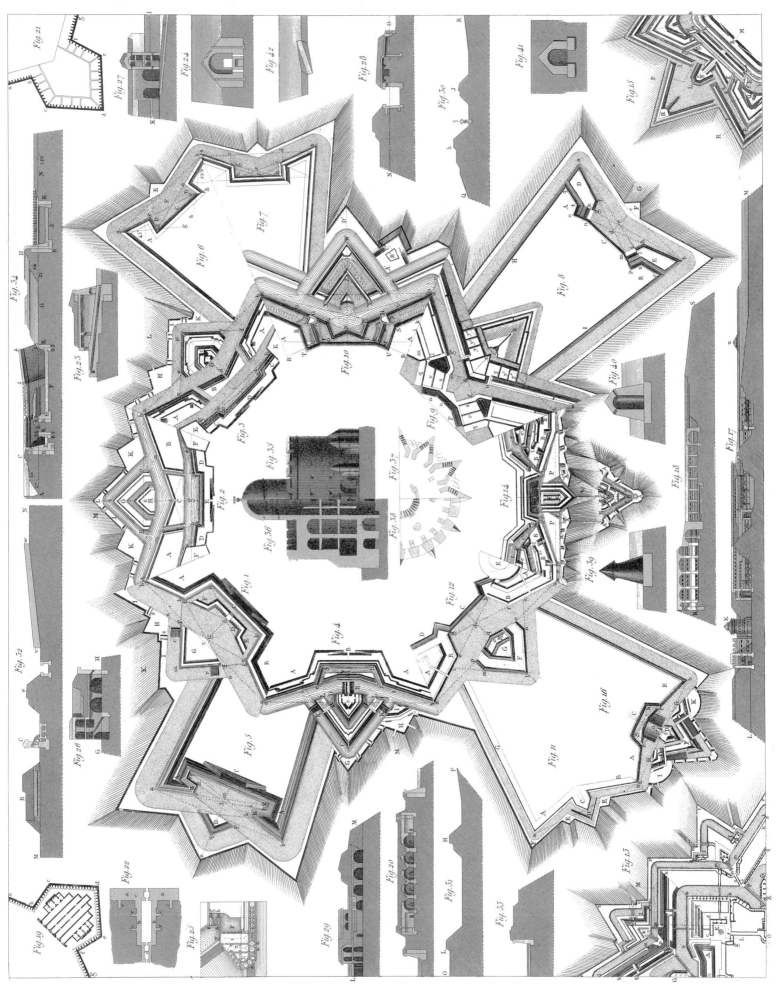

174

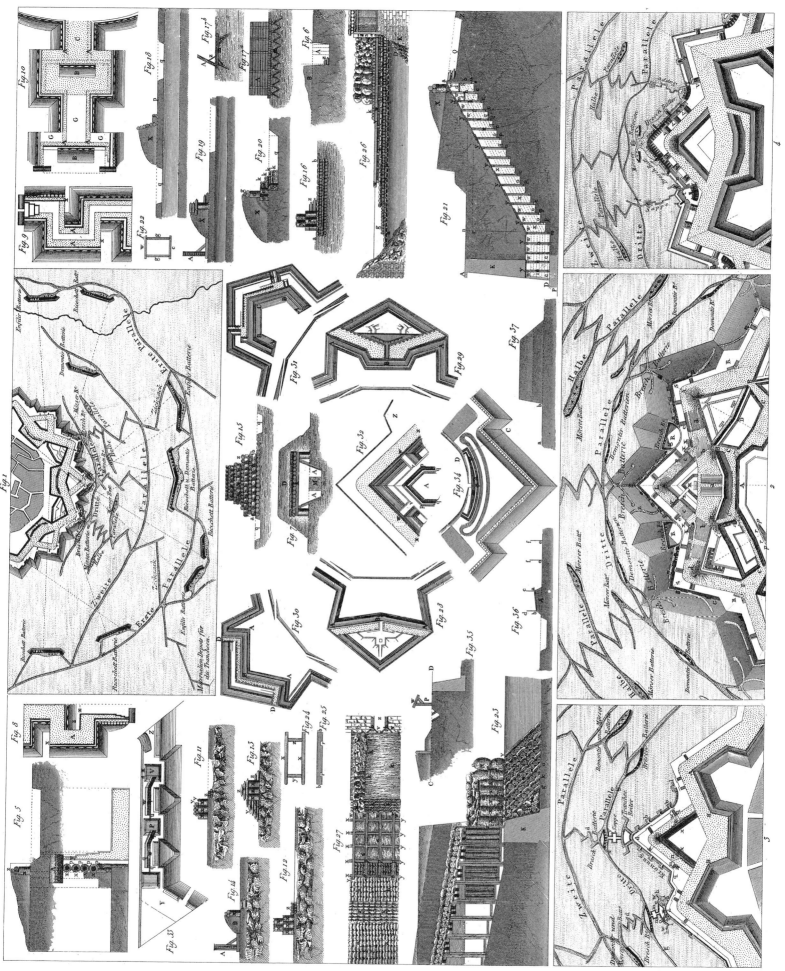

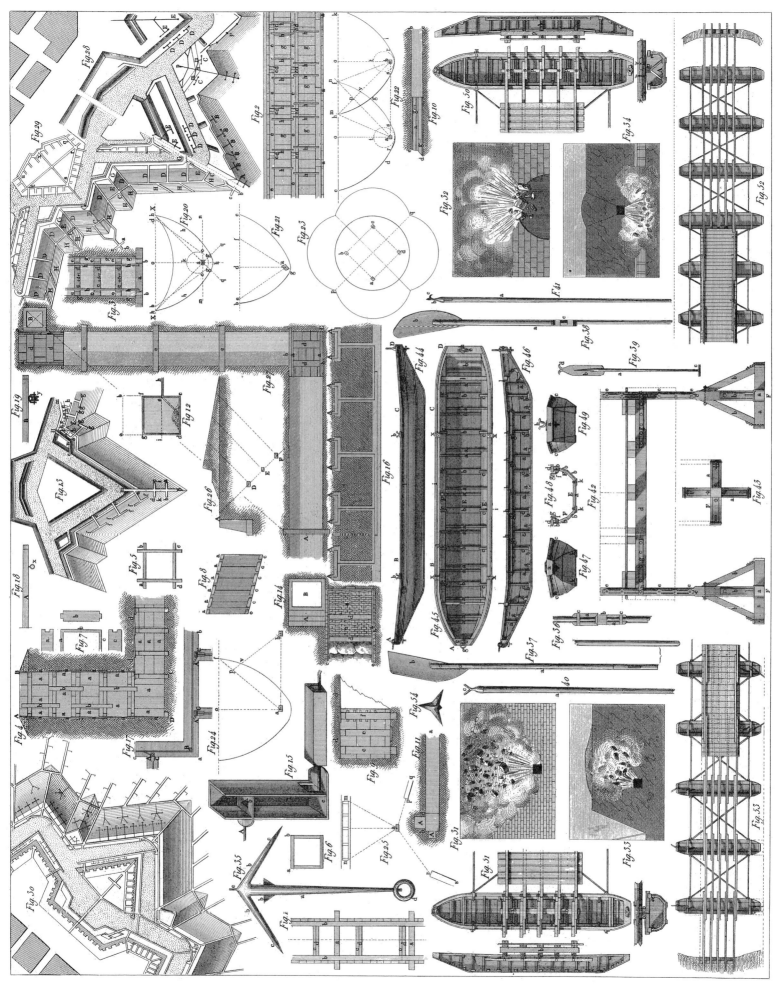

Military Sciences, Plate 51

Military Sciences, Plate 51 was the last Military Sciences plate. Nothing has been omitted.

Naval Sciences, Plate 1

179

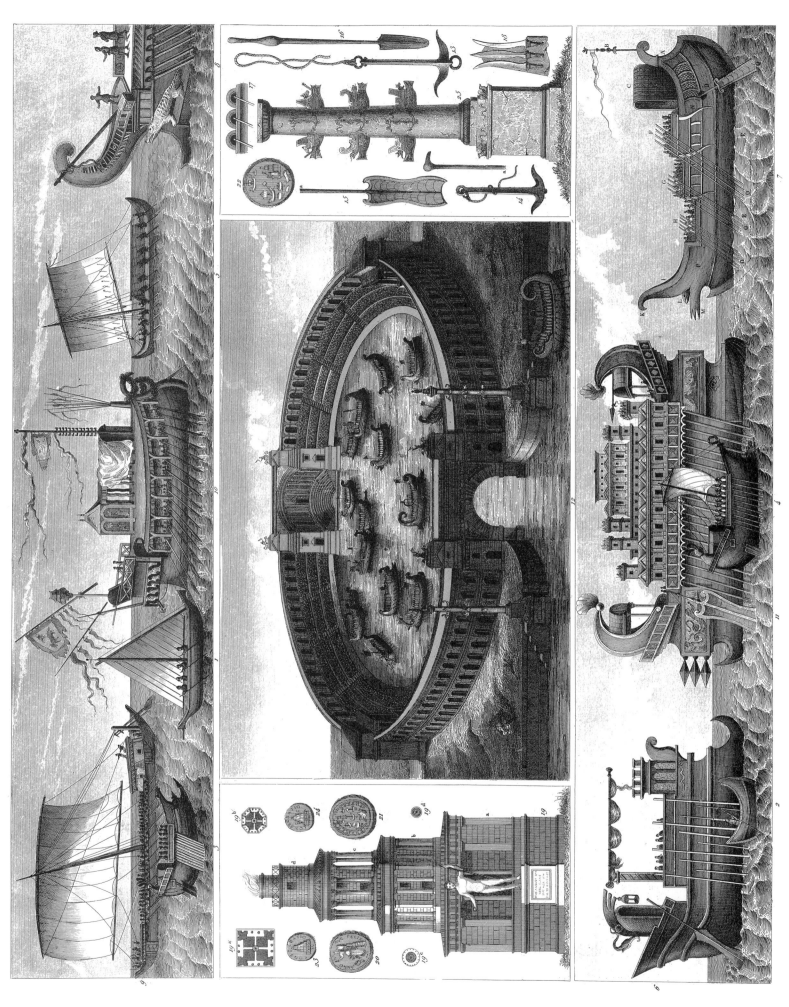

Naval Sciences, Plate 2

Naval Sciences, Plate 3

Naval Sciences, Plate 4

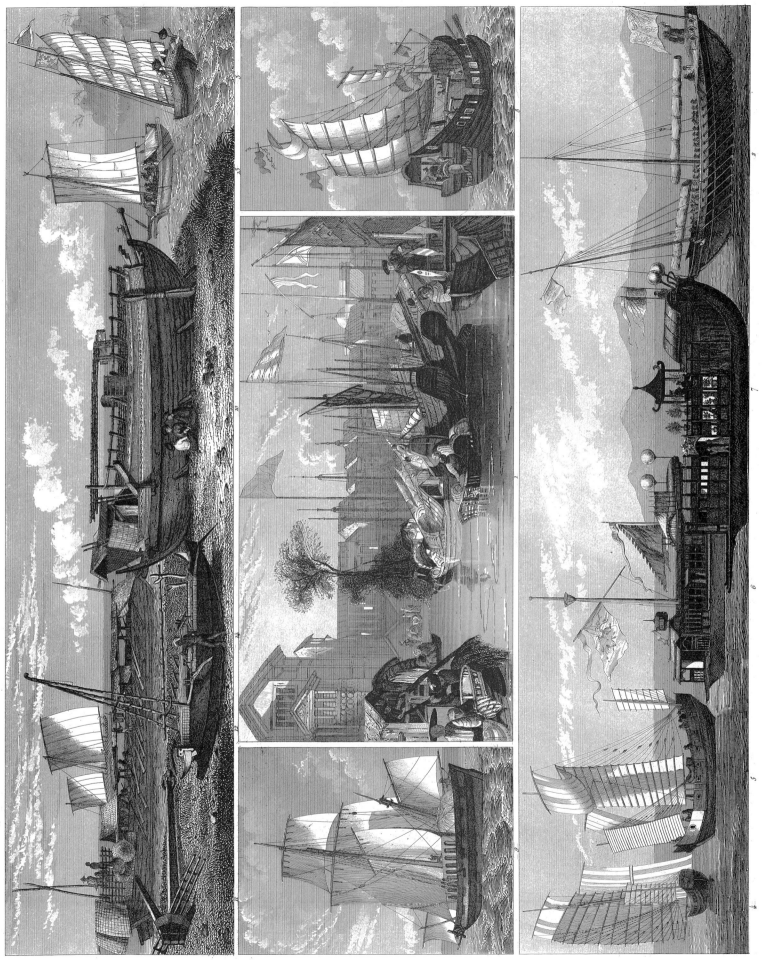

Naval Sciences, Plate 5

Naval Sciences, Plate 6

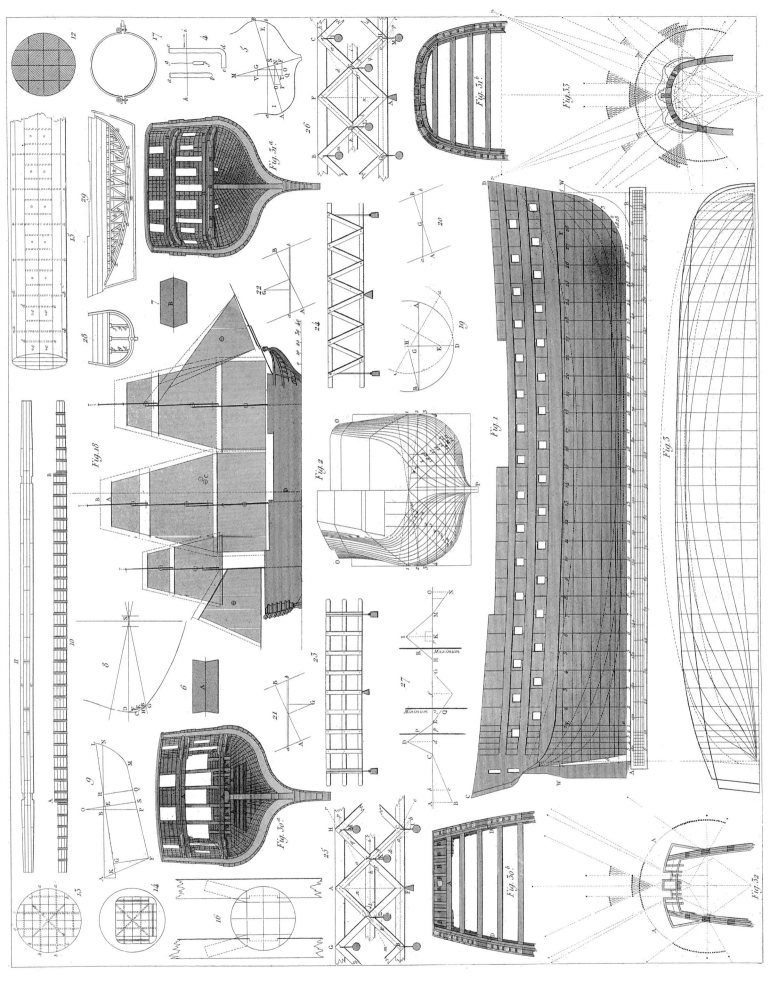

Naval Sciences, Plate 7

185

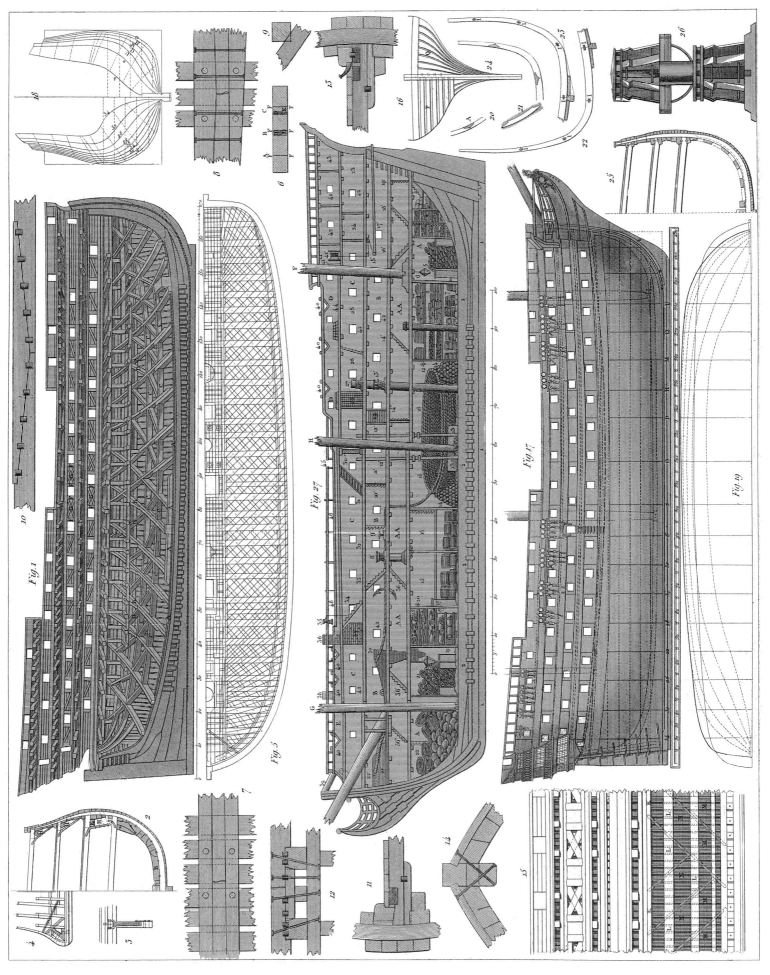

Naval Sciences, Plate 9

187

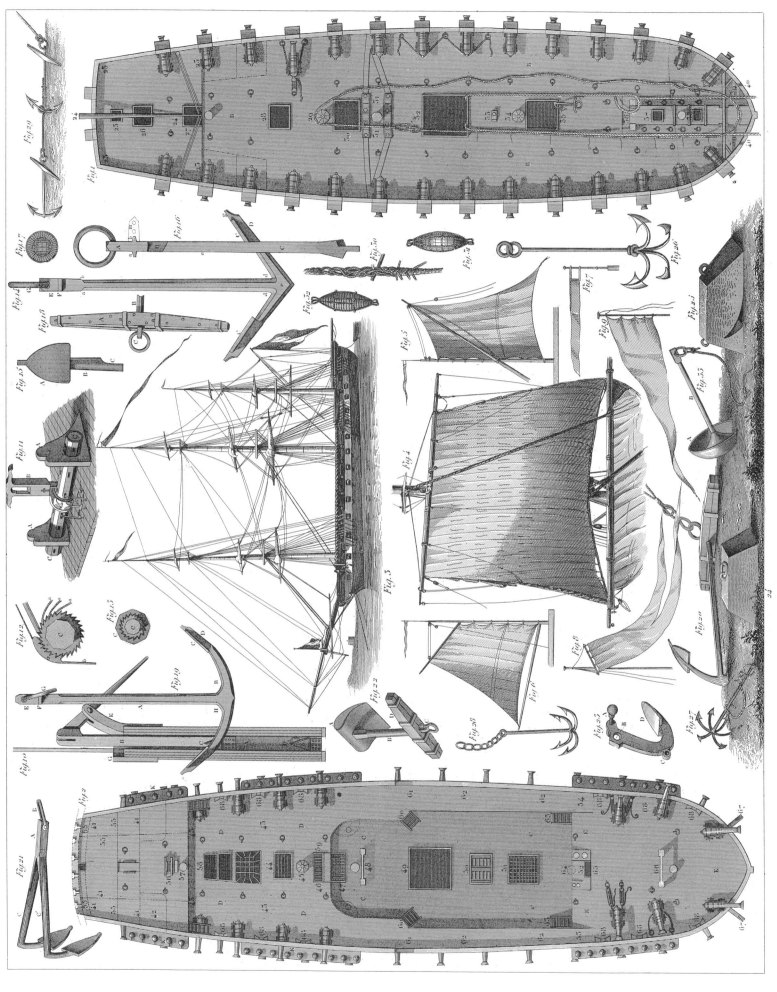

Naval Sciences, Plate 10

188

Fig.1

Naval Sciences, Plate 11

Naval Sciences, Plate 12

190

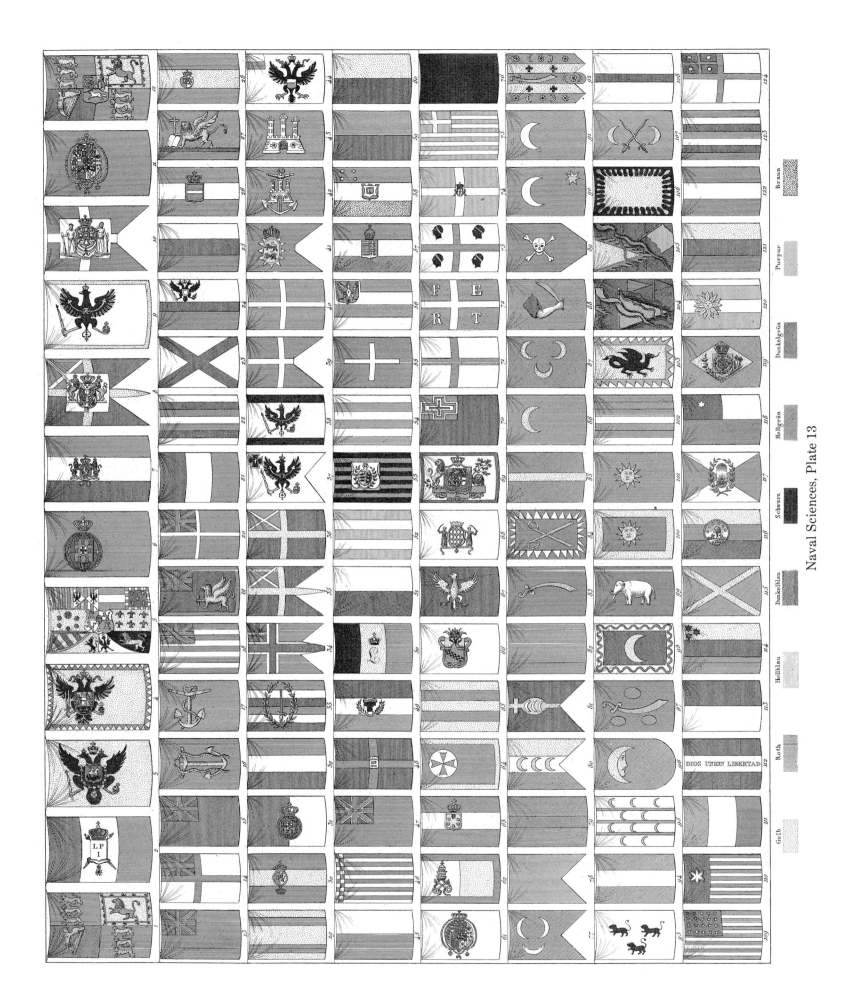

Naval Sciences, Plate 13

Braun
Purpur
Dunkelgrün
Hellgrün
Schwarz
Dunkelblau
Hellblau
Roth
Gelb

DIOS UNION LIBERTAD

191

Naval Sciences, Plate 14

Naval Sciences, Plate 15

Naval Sciences, Plate 16

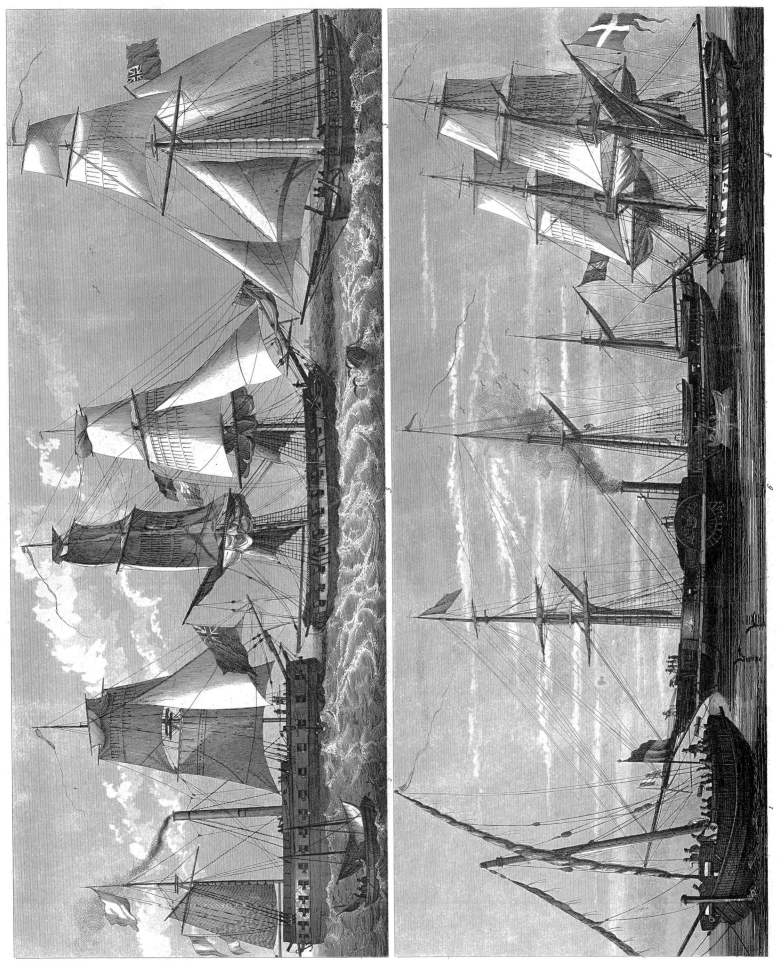

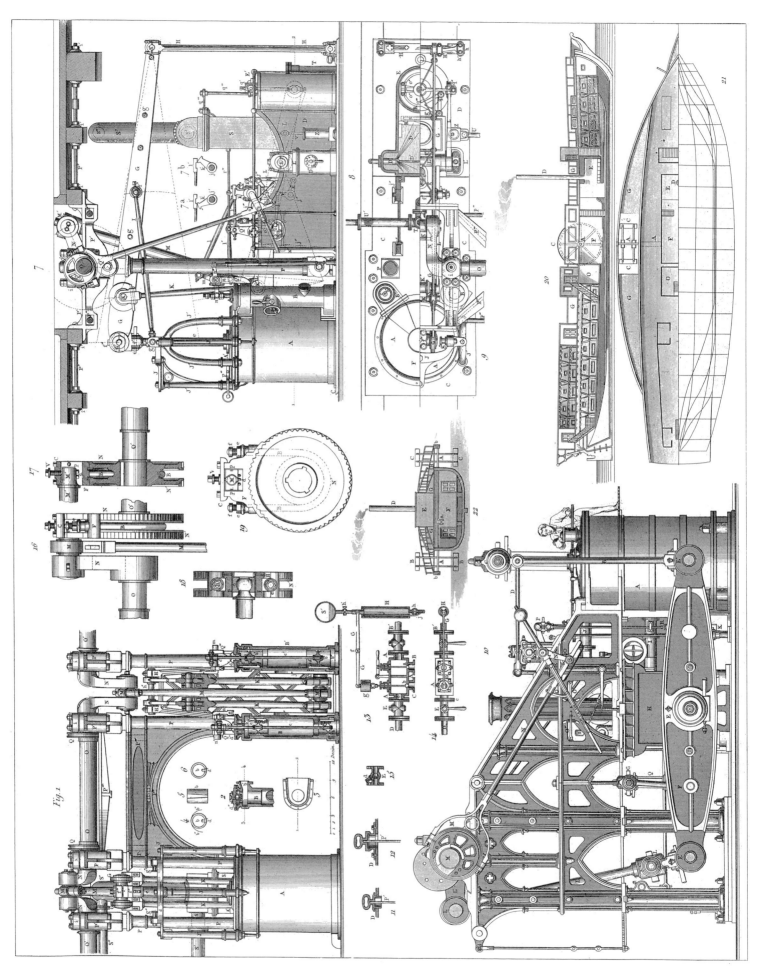

Naval Sciences, Plate 20

Naval Sciences, Plate 24

Naval Sciences, Plate 26

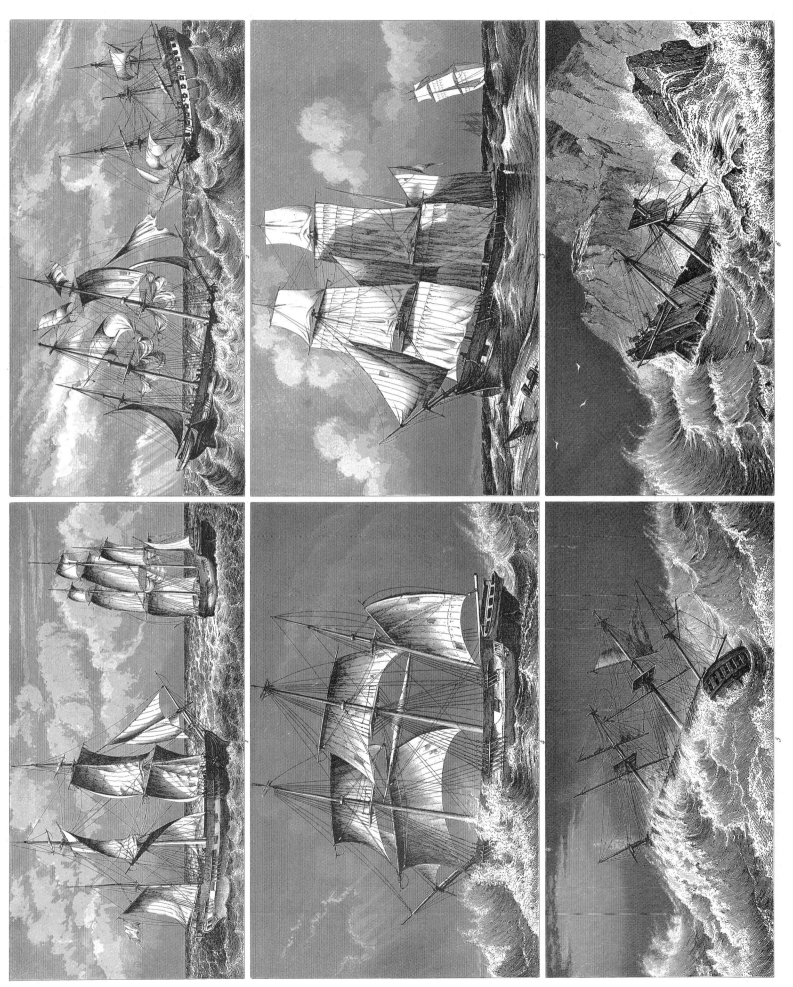

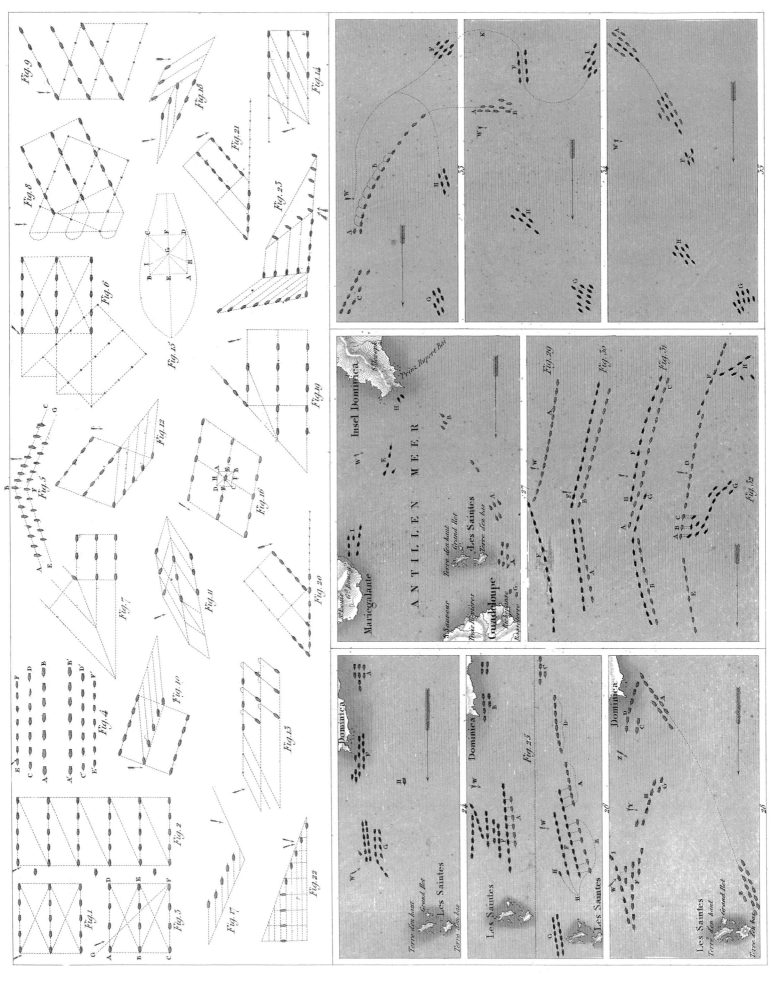

Naval Sciences, Plate 28

206

Naval Sciences, Plate 29

207

Naval Sciences, Plate 30

Naval Sciences, Plate 32